ISBN: 978-1-7363649-9-4

Printed in the United States of America

JUST BE, *Chile!*

BY

NICOLE PAYNE

Preface

When everyday life turns into stories that can be encased between two book covers, you end up with the work you're holding in your hands now. What started out as a series of blog posts, which accumulated over the span of two-and-a-half years, is now a compilation of treasures in the pages to come.

These stories hold my life in them. They hold the lives of my family members, friends, and other loved ones who probably (at the point I'm writing this) don't even know much about their place in this book. Thinking back on why I started to blog my life, I recall hitting a point when my satisfaction with my day-to-day dynamics began to change within me.

I remember standing in the middle of my classroom by one of my favorite students as he sat at his desk. I thought, "I don't want to do this anymore" (teaching being the "this" to which I was referring). I had hit a patch when my feelings about my daily grind as a school teacher had begun to turn me off. And I'm not truly certain I can articulate this much better than I have. However, I can communicate that, from there, I began to ask God why I'd, all of a sudden, begun to, quite strongly, feel this way.

It seemed to mirror how I physically felt the morning I began to miscarry my first pregnancy back in 2010. I sat down at the table to eat my breakfast of four eggs (as I'd proudly begun to do since becoming pregnant), and when I realized I could only get halfway through my plate, I thought it was odd. It was as if my body was telling me I no longer needed to eat as much as I was used to eating because the baby I was growing was no longer alive to require it. Later on that day, I faced the realization of the reason behind my loss of appetite.

Well, standing in the middle of my classroom eight years later, it was that same feeling of disconnect—from what I'd been a part of and what had been a part of me for more than a decade—that I felt. It was as if a stream of running water had abruptly been shut off. My passion for what I was doing had left me.

And as I continually listened to what God had to say about my change of heart, I began to hear things about a shift. Things about resigning from my teaching job as I knew it. A shift that would allow me time and space to explore the meaning and thrust behind a business I had begun a few years prior. A business with a mantra of just being who you were created to be—nothing more, nothing less—and being "comfortable" with everything this entails.

So, on these pages, this message rests, sits, reverberates, sings, screams, and speaks ... each story, a quick-enough peek into what this has looked like in my life over the past few years. In these pages I share the uncomfortable and imperfect scenarios that have been teaching me how to just be. In these pages are the funny and quirky stylings of the way God gives me speech and expression. In these pages are the regular routines that my family and I go through—accompanied by the way this "regular" speaks volumes about a God who's exceptional when it comes to putting touches on "regular," making it masterful.

Who are we to refuse being who we've been made to be? This is the question that I believe, much of the time, separates the usable from the unusable, the in-sync from the out-of-sync. A masterpiece doesn't tell its creator that it's going to be anything other than what it's been fashioned to be. And it is the same with you, me, and every other individual walking this earth.

So, as you read this book, you're graced with the option of reading several stories at once, or a story today and another tomorrow. They are chronological, but they're also selectable. And once you find your favorites, you can always quickly turn to them and have a blast! Some of them even end with suggested songs to listen to in order to put a cherry on top of the experience.

I certainly enjoyed writing this, and I'm confident you'll enjoy reading it. If you already know me, you'll hear my voice as you read. If you're just meeting me, you'll learn my voice and the reason why I'm so passionate about the message here.

So, here it is ... this passion—which will forever guide my life—to be the individual I've been crafted to be ... this passion for everyone else to do the same. Why? Because the world waits for us to BE this ... Yes! We are the solution, and there's no more time to waste.

Just be, chile! Just be!

Aug 10, 2018 — *Entry 1* — 2 min read

Home State—Amazing God

It's amazing how God avails Himself to reveal what He wants us to know about Him and His attributes. My husband, Kwesi, our boys, and I just spent 13 days in my home state of Texas, with family, to celebrate my baby sister's wedding. What a great occasion it was! I almost don't want to try and go through, in detail, the reasons why it was so great, but I will give it a quick GO!

Nostalgia at Its Best

From seeing former high school volleyball teammates that I hadn't seen SINCE HIGH SCHOOL to, of course, spending time with both my mom's and dad's sides of the family, to just being on my home turf with the huge multiple-lane highways (on which one can travel at higher speeds than I've witnessed here on the East Coast), to visiting with friends and their families who were constants for me throughout my childhood into adulthood—it was fun-loving and inspiring all around.

When we went to one of my former churches with my stepdad on Sunday, I was overwhelmed with God's availability to us NO MATTER WHERE WE ARE—be it in our normal everyday lives, intermingled among the mundane and ordinary, or be it on vacation, thousands of miles away from our normal. Whether we worship at our home church or, after several years, at the church we attended when we were a child—He's available to us.

It was wonderfully refreshing to be welcomed, greeted, and loved by family I hadn't seen in years, friends of my mom, family members of my stepdad, and loooooong time family friends of my dad's side—some of whom hadn't seen me since I was a little girl. They all wore genuinely happy smiles and hugged me as if they'd been missing me, on a daily basis, since they last saw me. PLUS, they looked so well kept by the Lord. And even in that, I saw and experienced the goodness of God. He is so amazing.

God in All of It

In addition, the feedback Kwesi consistently gave me about how he enjoys being around my family (family members he's known since we were courting and those he'd never met before this trip) was truly encouraging because he opened up about the inspiring characteristics within my family that he longs to see in his own.

My bottom line (before this piece loses focus—if it hasn't already since my children are literally jumping around me as I type) is that as an adult having just visited what and whom I've known since I was a child, I am seeing how God has kept, and worked, and adjusted, and guided, and anointed, and loved on, and just been consistent throughout many lives connected to me up to this point. He has been present and active in my life and the lives of those I've known for many years. And if one pays attention, one will continue to witness His goodness and God-ness in all of it.

Aug 12, 2018 **Entry 2** *3 min read*

Quality Life with Others in Mind

My quality of life, and that of my loved ones, has been on my heart for a little while now. I think it's because motherhood has caused me to look at how one person's physical, mental, or spiritual condition has high potential in affecting the other members of the household.

The Practical Still Teaches

A very practical example of this is when my husband once came home from work with cold symptoms. It wasn't long before *my* throat began hurting. I started sneezing, and Asa's (our elder son who was our only child at the time) and my noses were running. On top of this, I was the last one of us three to completely get over the cold. So, at some point during the course of all of this, I thought that maybe if my husband had been more proactive in protecting his own body from the cold, he wouldn't have brought it home, and Asa and I wouldn't have caught it (I do recall that during the cold months, I often find myself lovingly reminding hubby that a coat and hat would kinda' sorta' almost a little bit be helpful to his health).

Within the same vein regarding health and quality of life, beyond illnesses as minor as the common cold, are physical conditions that are quite major and all too common, due to the way we choose to treat our bodies—or better yet—our whole selves. As I age, I take note of how more than one life is affected by a health setback within a family. Now, I do understand the need to come to terms with caring for each other as we age naturally. I also understand caring for those affected by illnesses that the ill did not, so-to-speak, bring upon themselves through making unhealthy choices. However, when we are careless with ourselves as it pertains to eating habits, drug habits, mental habits, sexual appetite, and whatever else, we put our health at risk and set others (namely those closely connected to us) up to have to deal with the consequences of our poor choices.

Do I Have the Right?

I have half joked with my husband and extended family members, informing them that I would be a bit perturbed with them if they were to leave life on this side of heaven due to illness or depleted quality of life brought on and perpetuated by poor life decisions. And they have the right to have the same sentiment when it comes to me and the life choices I make. Simply because I love them so dearly, I don't want them to slight themselves of a quality life; I want them to live according to God's purpose, not dishonoring Him or themselves with respect to the time they have to serve this purpose.

I am confident that we can trust *Him* with our holistic health, but I am humbled in my humanity and the capability that He has given *me* to make wise choices concerning my health. And so, in this piece are no facts or figures—just heartfelt concern. Let's do our best to abandon ourselves, our desires, our wants, and our proclivities in exchange for asking God about what He wants for us in our ways of thinking, doing, and just ... being.

King David says it best in Psalm 139:23 & 24, when he writes:

"Search me, O God, and know my heart;
Try me, and know my anxieties;
And see if there is any wicked way in me,
And lead me in the way everlasting."

*I wrote this piece in 2014, but it still carries a theme that deserves perpetuating. Thus, I modified it, making it a tad more current.

Aug 15, 2018 **Entry 3** *4 min read*

A Bee Line Toward Peace

The Apostle Paul writes of having been all things to all men. Shoot! That's what I feel like at the moment as Kwesi, my mom-in-law, our sons, and I venture up to NY for a few days.

I often weigh the odds around which role I prefer playing on a road trip—the driver, whose concerns are driving safely, not getting a ticket, and maybe stopping for gas—or the front seat passenger who's in charge of handing out the snacks, supplying the napkins for clean-up, receiving the trash, running the in-car audio and video entertainment system, and applying slight or urgent pressure to the passenger side's imaginary break when the driver gets too close to the car in front of yours ... not to mention the whole process of thinking around packing up a family of four—two of whom are under the age of 12 (those of you with families larger than four, I'm not offended that you're rolling your eyes at me). Add to this a whiny three-and-a-half year-old who can't seem to understand that nap time has been stood up, and he and EVVVVVVERBODY else is PAYING FOR IT.

Hammy Mode

As we prepared to leave and lock up the house, I opted to hit my HAMMY MODE button in order that I would not LOSE MY MIND and spazz. Hammy is the over-excited, speed-of-light moving squirrel in the movie *Over the Hedge* who, in one scene, is sent over a hedge separating a wooded area from a residential area where, of course, humans live. He's sent over this hedge with the task of disarming the anti-vermin red laser alarm system in the front yard of a neighborhood homeowner association president. The plan is for Hammy to shut off the lasers so he and his posse of forgers can break into this overkill president's house and steal her food.

Hammy is given just a swallow of soda, which amps him to a level of heightened ridiculousness, and he begins to race, pinball style, hither and yon between various assigned posts in the yard in order to somehow beat the lasers so he can shut them off. To drive the point of Hammy's quickness home to the viewer, DreamWorks shows Hammy, in the midst of the pace of all things around him, taking a pleasant stroll through this crazy president's yard, seemingly unaware that he's in a life-threatening situation, in which he can get all his fur singed off by the demon red laser beams set up to not only trap vermin, but to decapitate and cage them. Hammy wears this dumb looking smile on his face—with his buck teeth resting on the outside of his mouth—and is just as happy as pie, not bothered by the reality around him.

Just Tryin' to Leave!!!

THIS, friends, is the mode I selected to jump right into as Kwesi and I moved busily outside of our home, packing the luggage, kids, and car up to leave for NY. Now, I could have gotten mad at the unmet expectation of pushing out earlier than we managed. I could have chosen to stay locked in CRAZY after telling my crying child to STOP IT and my older child to SHUT UP, as he decided to provide commentary play-by-play of what the crying child was doing. However, I'm working on abandoning myself and my flawed ways of doing things for how God wants me to handle things.

So, by the time we got to the end of the street, I had slipped into Hammy mode. I was resting in the fact that the chaotic *had* happened, was certainly at arm's reach, and was ready to push in on me from all sides at any moment. But I decided to take a ride of obliviousness, in the peace afforded me through the knowledge that truly, I had nothing to complain about. After the sweat down my back, the constant bending in and out of the un-air-conditioned car (which was not running yet) I had to do in order to get the kids' DVD system and earbuds sitchoo JUST PERFECT, and the fact that I felt Kwesi's frustration (which I could have chosen to take personally), I remembered the advice given by a friend for all seasons. She told me that there's a split second in which we can choose between what's right and what's wrong. There's a way of escape—ALWAYS—that God gives His people so that they choose the right thing.

Him over Me

I remembered that these days, and those ahead, I will live in abandonment of me for HIM. I want life's circumstances to always find me at the point where the muscle memory of my faith disappoints the dark expectations of my enemies. When I have the choice, I want it to be the God one. And here's the even cooler part–when I fail to make the God choice, God sees me and is not surprised or anxious. Therefore, I refuse to take on the anxiety that trying to be perfect definitely brings (and shame on me for ever trying).

I am appreciative to God for His nature of assurance. And I, as one of His children, reap the benefit of having this very same nature in *me.* I capitalize on it and rest in the serenity that it can never actually be snatched from me (though I could choose to give it up through my thought life and what I allow into my heart).

Francesca Battistelli writes about needing the Lord because the crazy *will* kick in. I am of the same mind.

Aug 23, 2018 — Entry 4 — 3 min read

Thank You for Wynter, God

I don't even know if I will live another moment. This car that I'm in right now with my family could encounter a drunk driver or be a part of a tragic eight-car pile-up on I-95. One or none of the four of us could or could not survive the crash. Does thinking like this make your skin crawl? It makes *mine* crawl.

However, this horrifying scenario makes the brevity of life no less real. I've been mulling over this since I got married 12 years ago, when I began to consider how closely attached another person's life is to mine—thinking about stuff like who will die first—my husband or me? I've been contemplating the vapor-like quality of life even more so within the past month.

Wynter's Passing

On July 25th this year, when I learned of the passing of 38-year-old Wynter Pitts—beautiful wife, mom of four (her oldest daughter played Danielle Jordan in the movie *War Room*), author, speaker, and blogger— I was taken aback, to say the least. As far as I know, she did not experience an elongated illness. According to her family, she stopped breathing and that was it. Wow ...

I believe this hit me hard because:

- Wynter was the niece of Dr. Tony Evans—well-known founder and pastor of Oak Cliff Bible Fellowship in Texas. I follow his children closely because I admire and am inspired by them. Not only do I respect what they're doing in God's kingdom, but I'm close in age with them and went to the same high school, summer camps, and after school programs as some of them. I feel some sort of connection with *them* even if they don't remember *me.*
- Wynter left a husband and four blossoming girls—all under the age of 15—behind.
- Wynter was the age that I just turned a few days ago.
- This was so sudden. I mean, she was alive and then she wasn't. Her heart ... stopped.

The Hope That Matters

On the other side of this token, what's breath-taking is the strength with which her immediate and extended family are responding. Her husband, Jonathan, writes, *"We are heartbroken and in much pain, but we rest in the hope that we have in* ***Jesus Christ*** *... So if Wynter's life and sudden passing teaches you anything,* ***learn to live every day in light of that fact.****"*

What fact? The fact that there is **HOPE** to be had in **JESUS** and **KNOWING HIM.** And this is not a cliche' or bandwagon talk; I KNOW what I'm talking about. I've had my own heartbreak, issues, and trials as I've learned of the goodness and God-ness of God. I've experienced miscarriage and scary diagnoses, a car spinning out of control on a busy highway with my husband and me in it, and so on. And even if you're reading this knowing that you've experienced way worse, it doesn't make the track record that God has created for Himself in my own life obsolete. What it does is makes it obvious that God not only has a track record in one person's life, but He has a track record that *supersedes* just one life and sits high for all to see.

When it comes to the fragility of our existence and what Jonathan Pitts wants people to learn from Wynter and her unexpected death, the true tragedy is when one dies *not knowing* **JESUS** as the forgiver of his sin. This is because when you don't know **CHRIST**, you're playing Russian Roulette with the whisper of life that we know on this side of eternity. When your time is up here, and you find yourself not having accepted **CHRIST** into your heart, you're a **goner**–forever. There is no hope of life for you after death, like there is for the Christian.

John 11:25 says, *"Jesus said to her (Martha when her brother Lazarus had died), I am the resurrection and the life. He who believes in Me, though he may die, he shall live."*

More Freedom

Wynter's death has introduced me to a new level of freedom. This is the putting away of time wasters—nursing a bad attitude that's not worth having, allowing fear to immobilize me or anxiety to taunt me, choosing the ridiculous pace of life over soundness within my family, loafing on God and not letting Him get out of me what He knows He put in me—just making the wrong call on what really matters.

My next moment is not a luxury that I'm certain to have. So, I best get to living in the light of this.

I thank God that the death of His saints carries a glory that erases lethargic living.

Thank You for Wynter, God.

Sep 1, 2018 — *Entry 5* — 4 min read

Get Back Right!

I came to my chiropractor so he can fix me. Gotta' get my back right after injuring it—almost a year and a half ago—squatting heavy weight in the gym.

After college (about 16 years ago), I became quite concerned (with seasons of obsession) about maintaining the athletic body I had as a college athlete. When I played volleyball for Morgan State, I was *told* what to do with my body, in the athletic department's hopes that I wouldn't waste its scholarship money so that I'd produce the athleticism it hoped I'd produce. My teammates and I were put on strength and conditioning programs, underwent two-a-day practices, and were provided food *on* campus *and* when we went away for matches. These mandatory things caused me to have a certain body that I liked but failed to appreciate then the way I do now. Part of this is because I was younger, not having the responsibilities *or* freedom I have now.

With this freedom, I can go to the gym or not; I can eat right or not; I can ensure that I'm doing the things to maintain or maximize my health or not. And it has taken me some time since college to mature in my perspective on my body and health, but I believe God is okay with how I see it now. I believe this because the announcement of a church fast no longer makes me cringe or cry on the front row (a shoulder bouncing type of cry). I no longer go to the gym to beef up so that my thighs and butt turn men's heads or pull envious attention from other women. I now work out in order to stay fit, strong, and healthy because God gave me this body and I'm supposed to make choices about it that show Him I appreciate what He's done in making me.

It's like this ... as a school teacher, many times a thought to purchase something for my classroom is only a fleeting one because I've experienced the way young people in my building have not shown respect for what educators' thoughtfulness and resources have provided them. And because I sacrifice—on a daily basis—to earn my money, I get angry when someone else misuses or destroys what I've purchased with it. I imagine that my misuse of my body, in any way, has projected the same message of disregard and disrespect toward God.

So, here I am at my chiropractor's office to fix what I injured in my back while trying to look like I did in college. Yes, I'm undergoing physical correction with each visit, but it reminds me of how God takes the time to correct what we've messed up in ourselves *spiritually* in order to prepare us for things He knows we need prepping for.

The Pressure Points

On a normal chiropractic visit, the first thing that happens is I lie on my stomach on a special table that's made for adjusting patients. I'm told to take in a deep breath and then exhale as my chiropractor strategically applies pressure from the top down to the bottom of my back. As he does this, I must lie there and trust that he knows what he's doing while applying this heavy pressure on a very sensitive area of my body—an area that stabilizes me. It is much like this in my spiritual walk. I must trust God as He applies strange pressure to areas of my life that will, after He's corrected them, stabilize me as a representative of His way of doing stuff. This pressure—on which He signs off—in my life is not comfortable, nor does it ever feel convenient. But it's necessary for correction.

Don't Resist the Twists

The next step my chiropractor takes is instructing me to turn on my side—putting my top knee over my bottom one and folding my arms so he can twist my body in a way that produces audible cracking noises—several of them. He does the other side in the same manner. This position could be a frightening one if I did not trust that he knows what he's doing and has my best interest at heart. Likewise, the Lord puts me in seemingly twisted situations and trials that I could get bent out of shape about if I was not aware of the fact that He knows I'm ready for such testing and twisting. It is here that I'm humbled because I have to let Him shift my perspective, or else I'll become a casualty of my own understanding.

Beauty in the Blind Side

The last thing my chiropractor does is tell me to lie on my back. Then, he abruptly, but skillfully, twists my head to the right once, then the left (several cracks again), and after, pulls my head toward his body as he stands behind me (seemingly stretching my neck). In like manner, I've experienced God abruptly dropping things, events, and conditions into my life that have rocked my world as I knew it, but later revealed the beauty in how the blind-siding factor of the trial skillfully equipped me with greater awareness of Him and the peace that He is—no matter what kind of chaos I'm in.

It's an Adjustment

Get this. A chiropractic adjustment is strange—awkward at first—but once you start feeling the results of the pressing and twisting, you're grateful for the hands and expertise of your chiropractor. I cannot say that I've appreciated God's testing at its onset, but I now know what it means to consider it an opportunity for joy when trouble comes my way. "For you know that when your faith is tested, your endurance has a chance to grow. So let it grow, for when your endurance is fully developed, you will be perfect and complete, needing nothing" (James 1:3-4).

When I start to complain, indulging in feeling sorry for myself in trouble, my relationship with God and being attentive to His reminders that He's walking through life with me encourages my heart. He reminds me that He signs off on the hard stuff because He knows He'll get glory out of me through it. This helps me stick to my guns, and it always gets me back right.

Thank You, God.

Flapjacks and Faith

Somebody say, ***PANCAKES FOR DINNER***!

Isn't this the best??!!

In the opinion of a five-ingredient cookbook totin' mom like myself, and the three and seven-year-old kids who can eat pancakes at any point of the day and LOVE THEM, these fluffy flapjacks save the day many, many times in my household (like they did today for dinner).

Child, Teach!

It was my seven-year-old's brief commitment to whining this evening that reminded me of what I'm about to say. See, he had his mind set on an after-school snack because that's what he's used to when coming home each day. He eats a snack, does his homework, then waits for dinner. However, today I had a half-day at work (I'm a school teacher) and was able to get home and make the pancakes just before leaving to pick him up from school. So, as far as he knew, he was going to have to wait the normal amount of time for dinner to be ready; therefore, he dreamed of his usual before-homework snack.

In the car on the way home from school, when he asked me if he could have his snack once we got home, I told him no. And before I could decide if I wanted to give him the reason for my answer, he began to whine and moan. I then decided not to tell him about the pancakes.

Bigger than YOU

As more time passed today, I began to think about how we Christians do this to God when He says or does something that we don't like or agree with—when His decisions and mindset don't tickle our have-it-all-together fancies, and when we've decided that He needs to rethink His time table. We whine and complain to people who haven't quite figured out how to tell us to shut up about it, or we carry the victim/ unjustly treated mentality around with us. *Or* we simply keep thinking about how things would work so much better if they were the way we saw fit for them to be—not knowing what God's agenda is.

I once heard author and speaker Henry Blackaby say that we as Christians talk about "God's will **for my life.**" Mr. Blackaby went on to say that there's **JUST God's will**, and how we fit *into* it is what we should make our business. He stressed that living is about understanding that God's will is bigger than just YOU and ME, and that it's about how you and I live in abandonment of ourselves to His purposes—whatever they may be. Our scope should widen beyond our little world as we realize that the rest of the world is on God's agenda too. So, our question to

God becomes simplified. *God, what is Your will–period? What do I do?* Believe me. He knows where you and I fit in the grand scheme.

Today, my son got home and found that not only dinner, but one of his favorite dinners, was waiting on him. Thus, his tune changed abruptly. I'm learning, as God's child, that I want my tune to be consistent whether I get what I want, when I want it, or not. This way, I don't have to feel childish when things finally *do* end up working out for me pretty sweetly–only *after* I've whined my way through them or not shown God a good, trusting attitude.

So, Chilllll

He's introduced me to some hard things to show me I'm actually not as smart as I thought I was, and that I actually *don't* have that really dope glue to hold things together like I thought I did.

So, when my children show me their impatience and lack of understanding when it comes to who's in charge, I'm learning to sit back on the inside and know that I have nothing to be anxious about in my response to them. I know what they *don't* know, and I don't have to get out of sorts to show them this. My *God* has no reason to get out of sorts. Neither do I.

Sep 16, 2018 — **Entry 7** — *4 min read*

Can't Stay in My Feelings

Prove this! Fix data! Manage your classroom of challenging children! Fill this form out for under-performers! Call these homes for the truant kids! Attend this meeting for the climate issues and that meeting for Instructional Leadership! Show the district what they want to see! Catch all the kids who are on their phones during instruction! Keep every kid engaged in your lesson! Explain why that kid was sleeping in your class! Then go home, grade, and lesson plan when your work day is done!

Do I want to bow out? Yes–

After almost 15 years, I feel like I'm done with this urban teaching scene–the school teaching scene period. I'm convinced that I can actually live the rest of my life without doing another lesson plan, and–be–FINE.

I have a good teacher friend who, as this summer came to an end, wrote about her itch to get back to her students. I didn't share that same itch. In fact, my itch had more to do with dread, which I had to snatch and put away from me.

But I'm Grateful

Though I've had these thoughts and feelings in intense waves since about the middle of last school year, I do realize that I'm to be grateful for my teaching job. It's been my current source of income and one channel of God's provision to my family for just shy of 15 years. So, I won't spit on it with disdain; it's been a major contributor in giving my family the lifestyle of comfort and opportunity we've come to know. It's been consistent and dependable, and I thank God.

Also, God has put AND KEPT me on a spiritual post in my career, where He has groomed and conditioned me as an educator who knows Him—planting and watering seeds that He's already caused and will cause to bloom and grow for His glory and pleasure. Just like He's wanted and loved me over the years I've known Him, I know He wants and loves the students, families, and faculty I see on a daily basis. Again—thank You, Lord.

I Sense a Shift

It's been hard, grueling work—this is for sure—and I'm honored that God knew I'd operate out of the goods He gave me in my mother's womb to do what I've done in this one school for my entire career. I just really sense a shift in my world, and I believe that these feelings of *I'M RET TUH GO* have something to do with this shift.

So, though the start of this piece probably had you thinking, *What is going on with her?* I think the true message is becoming clear.

The GOD in me won't let me go too far into myself when I go through the temptation of emotionally throwing up my hands because I know how UNtrustworthy this part—this emotional part— of me is.

Here's where you find me—

I'm stronger.

During the daily seven-hour whirlwind of deadlines, quotas, and kids who need a whole lot of love, I look at myself and see that I've gained some muscle mass. I watch myself chill in the midst of the crazy. Though you may pass my classroom and see me looking busy—maybe even frantic sometimes—I'm a different kind of chick on the inside. And it's a very strange place to be because it's far from comfortable but right for the GIANT in me.

I now know the strange pleasure that maturing Christians can have in trial because we know it's perfecting, strengthening, and establishing us according to God's pattern of child rearing. This sweet spot gets really trippy when we can smile in the fire and wink at our enemies when we're hurting.

The Good Kind of Crazy

It's a Castor Troy (the movie *Face Off*) type of experience! When the pain's piled on, and our eyes get wild with the knowledge that we're thriving off of it instead of buckling under it, I offer that our enemies—THE enemy—freaks out even more because he finds that the crazy in trial brings out the crazy in us—God's peeps. This is the type of crazy that hinges on the uncovered posture of our audacious hunger to follow God, NO MATTER WHAT. The devil's schemes fall apart and backfire, leaving him in the dusty cloud of our continual turn to God.

So, yes, I'm excited about this shift (that I've been in prayer about and have solicited prayers from others regarding), but I'm grown enough to know that though the grass certainly looks greener on the other side of School Teacher, this DOES NOT change the fact that it'll still have to be mowed. My next chapter will have its own learning curves, growing pains, and muscle builders that'll show up in circumstances where my faith will continue to be tested. And I'll have to keep going then like I have over these years in the school system, which has been a conduit through which my Schoolmaster's pushed me toward spiritual beast-hood. And always a student, I really just want to be found paying attention and obedient.

Sep 24, 2018 — **Entry 8** — 3 min read

Put in My Place

Is it just me, or do *you* approach anxiety when you feel time running away from you? Is this just a woman thing or a human thing? I often have to remind myself to chill when I start to give way to frenzy, fully aware of ALL that MUST get done. Oh geez, chile.

One evening just last week, I told my husband that I physically felt I was wound too tightly. I felt like one of those wind-up toys that someone had just wound, making it ready to hit any surface and run. But the thing was that it was evening, and the work day had already passed. I was actually supposed to be chillin' with my husband, but I remember lying down on the bed to relax, and my mind was still racing, coupled with my head feeling as tight and as tense as ever.

Hubby actually ended up unloading some eye-opening information on me. And after he left the room, I cried my eyes out. He pretty much told me about how I'm so Busy Betty about everything but the stuff I don't want to do. He told me that some of what I'm busy doing shouldn't take as much priority as I'm giving it. He told me about how our family takes a back seat to some of these other priorities much of the time. He told me of how I neglect to pay attention to some of the things he says and that I end up doing the opposite more than not–hard stuff to hear, I tell ya'. I ain't feel good at all when he was finished. And I was frustrated that his words didn't match up with what I wanted to hear. However, I've noticed that we're stronger for it.

Since that "session," I've tried to be more intentional about "doing" for my family and home BEFORE I "do" for my job and our new business. I'm trying to be a more effective listener to him and my children, purposing to silence distractions while they're talking–not mentally planning out my next few minutes, days, or hours–but for real being in the moment with them–being present. This goes right along with one of my previous pieces in honor of what Wynter Pitts' unexpected passing is teaching me.

I don't want to rely on learning on a curve. I want to take counsel, apply it, and see the fruit of my application. As I tend to be a person of action, I don't like to wait until tomorrow to do what I have the time to do today. However, I *am* learning, as a maturing child of God, that there is a line drawn between frantic activity and responsible productivity. If I'm not wise, I easily slip and slide, teetering back and forth between the two.

But–

Where can I go from Your Spirit?
Or where can I flee from Your presence?
If I ascend into heaven, You are there;
If I make my bed in hell, behold, You are there.
If I take the wings of the morning,
And dwell in the uttermost parts of the sea,
Even there Your hand shall lead me,
And Your right hand shall hold me.

Psalm 139 says it well. Regardless of what goes on in my life, my God is with me. Not only is He with and for me, but He is IN me, putting in my heart the desires He knows I should have. So, what's the point of being an agitated, frantic wreck?

He has made me productive—this I know. And I will not allow life to dictate to me what my priorities should be. My Lord does this, and I'm so thankful to my husband for being His mouthpiece that night of the hard talk. I don't mind being reminded of my place because if I play my cards right, I won't frustrate the grace of a God who chooses to speak to me through others.

Truth Ain't Gonna' Change

If your life is driven by your five senses,
you are not a mature Christian.

Are you picking your face up off the floor?

Take your time.

This was a chin-checking statement for me too, considering that my emotions have been going through whirlwind-like channels over this last season in my life.

Emotions Don't Have the Final Say

Dr. Tony Evans, who said the thing above about being an immature Christian, also said that angels aid God's people, and that even though a believer is having a difficult time in life, the angels are there ministering–helping, [not judging our emotions].

I sometimes go through yielding to condemnation for feeling fearful, angry, sad, frustrated, or hopeless. But I believe I miss the mark when I hang my righteousness on condemnation around what I *feel.* This is because the only true difference between my best and worst days is my response to what's true—not what I feel.

Not Spilled Milk, But ...

My three-year-old spilled some orange juice on the dining room floor today after my time at school—where I'd been caged (did I say *caged?*) with my foul-mouthed, disengaged, energy-sapping students [that I'm praying for daily] for hours.

My seven-year-old, whose orange juice it was, started to "lose it" after the cup hit the floor. Since I was on the verge of losing it myself (needing to hit my after-school reset button so my own kids would have a fighting chance), I decided to verbalize to both of my boys that it was okay that the juice was spilled, that it was an accident, that we all have JESUS in our hearts and would be fine, and that (arriving to screaming at the top of my lungs) *"GOD IS STILL GOOD! HALLELUJAH!"*

Can you picture this?

Can you hear me yelling??!!

If you know me well, you probably can.

I figured that, versus yelling to express the frustration I really felt at the time because of what I'd just left at school, I would speak age-appropriate encouragement to my sons and scream praises to God so my emotions wouldn't get the best of me (because I sho could've yelled something else).

Mason-Dixon

I believe that herein lies the Mason-Dixon line of spiritual maturity. I may have looked and sounded like a fool, but I threw the devil a curveball with which he couldn't connect. The Bible says that God uses foolish things to throw the wise. He also gives us the ability to praise Him in order to confuse our enemies. So, even though I felt a little crazy in the moment, and my three-year-old asked me why *I* was shouting, I wasn't the one confused, and the "crazy" felt kind of good.

Currently, weighing probably about a buck 10 (on a 21-day church-wide fast), I feel **big** on the inside and am coming to the end of caring too much about what things look like. I'd rather concern myself with the truth, which my feelings can't change.

Thank You, Lord, that my weaknesses are Your sweet spots!

"My grace is sufficient for you, for my power is made perfect in weakness."
"Therefore I will boast all the more gladly about my weaknesses, so that Christ's power may rest on me."
- 2 Corinthians 12:9 (NIV)

Sep 29, 2018 — Entry 10 — 3 min read

I'm Good, Regardless

Ever been a front passenger in a car that comes to an abrupt stop to avoid hitting the car in front of you, but you're afraid to show how frantic this abrupt stop makes you because the driver catches an attitude if you show just *how* frantic the abrupt stops make you?

I'm like "WHAT!? I CAN'T BE CONCERNED ABOUT SAFETY AND LIFE???!!! GEEZ! A SISTA' CAN'T CARE IF SHE LIVES OR DIES?"

Too specific?

You know what I'm talkin' bout?

You know the type of driver I'm referring to?

I'm just sayin.

But what I can also say, on the same day of the abrupt stop in the car (LOL), is something about the next scenario:

Passenger Seat's Not SO Bad

Our family of four arrived home after a morning errand. We were still sitting in the car, and Kwesi (hubby) was making some mental notes about what needed to be done in the house before we all got out of the car. In a few moments, he told Asa (our older son) to put his seat belt back on. Then Asaiah (our younger son) started repeatedly asking about where we were going. At this point, *I* didn't even know because Kwesi had *just* made this decision. After about the third time Asaiah asked the same question, I turned to him and said, "Dad knows, and that's enough; just ride." Kwesi drove us to the park so the boys could play outside on that really nice day.

Pull on Him

The late Dr. Myles Munroe, sensational preacher and orator, advised wives to tug on their husbands' capacity to lead the home through questioning about his vision and plans (since we are fashioned to be his help meet). I love this advice and the fruit it yields because God put in me, as a woman, a need to be covered, guarded, and guided by a man. When I was single, the man responsible for this was my dad. When I got married, the responsibility shifted to Kwesi. And through it all—singleness and marriage—GOD has been the CONSTANT Keeper.

I'll Take "WOMAN" for $300 Please, Alex!

I say, all the time, that I'm glad God didn't make me a man because I don't want his responsibility and role of leading the family, being the one who has to answer to God for how we turn out, collectively and independently (I actually need to keep hubby in prayer more because of how loaded his call really is). I want to be the beautifully exquisite, godly woman that I am—knowing my own role and capacity to dynamically do what God wants me doing—being who He wants me being.

So, I was excited inside to know nothing of the destination Kwesi had decided on from the driveway of our home. He made the call, and it made me glad to tell my son we didn't need to know the destination. Dad—our leader—knew, and that was enough.

Even in my cares about my life, my safety, and that of my husband and kids (abrupt stop scenario at the beginning of this piece), I've learned to, right after rolling my eyes accompanied by my pulsating heart, breathe and trust that God's got us. Our FATHER knows our destination and everything between there and now.

Can't Touch This

There's a princess type of feeling I have while resting in my privilege to be looked after, cared for, maintained, pruned, and made better by my heavenly Dad, Comforter, Guard, and Guide. You really can't touch me even if you harm me.

Live or die, I'm secured in WHOSE I am. Without this security in Christ, I'd be doomed— whether I had millions of dollars in the bank and pristine health or whether I was penniless—scraping by just to physically function at all. Only the Christian is truly untouchable, rain or shine, hungry or full, mad or naw. And I'm just glad I'm on the right train.

It's cuh-raaazy what God can do with you through a perspective shift. Yowzers!

Oct 2, 2018 Entry 11 *3 min read*

Caution—Get Someplace Where You Can Scream!

Mrs. Deborah asked me, "Where were you 30 years ago?" I laughed and told her I was eight years old. Her inquiry came right after she told me about how she's loving the material I'm writing. I appreciate, so very much, this feedback from readers young to old and back again.

The fact that she asked me where I was almost 80% of my life ago tells me she believes she could've used the messages I write *now* back when *she* was a young wife and mom. And this further confirms some things my pastor has prophetically spoken to me about wisdom's role in my life and the way this wisdom will affect others—specifically women.

I'm enjoying being on this journey and in this season where my pen feels like it's on fire—a blazing one because of what I've seen God take me through, cause me to triumph over, and show me has no parts with me. He's proven to me that He knows what He's talking about, that His Word really is the truth, that He, for real, has made me more than a conqueror, and that truly I *am* a creation just a notch down from the angels—who—I know have been assigned to me to help me navigate life.

Try This on for Size

Now, check out this God-given food for thought I received just before my lunch break today.

If you know you're in a Job type of season—one in which you did nothing wrong to bring the chaos and spiritual warfare that's seized your world (but you actually did something *right*)—try this way of thinking on for size:

1. God decided to lift His hedge that once surrounded you.
2. He did this because He KNEW that THROUGH this, you would let Him pull out the warrior He put in you when He wrought you.
3. If GOD'S allowed this, why are you ashamed of the fight? Because of what others will think and say?
4. This really *was* a set-up! God knew you would kick Satan's tail all up, down, and through this camp as you learn the ropes of this level of warfare!

And with this train of thought, I realize that I done stepped into another weight class! I'm wiser, more anointed, more DANGEROUS, having turned my attention to my Father in greater ways than before! I now see JUST HOW IMPORTANT HE IS, JUST HOW "**DONE**" SATAN REALLY IS, AND HOW MUCH POWER IS IN MY OBEDIENCE.

So, no longer am I focused on the fact that an abrupt shift took place regarding what I knew spiritual warfare to be.

No longer am I focused on the fact that I don't like it.

I've shifted my perspective and have gotten cozy with the fact that there's a bullseye on my back that I'm gonna' live with as a soldier in God's army! And you know what? I now know fear's assignment. It's to paralyze, immobilize, torment, and torture. And I realize I AIN'T DOWN WIT THAT!

Loo-Hoo-Zer-Her!

Ha! Satan! YOU ... LOSE! I'm always armed now and will forever be dangerous to you and yours. Even if you touch me, you can't *really* touch me! But you knew this.

It's taken *me* some time to find out, but now I see why this season has been sooooo hard. It's because this is where I'll make the altar called NOW I KNOW! And I'll make my own altar calls when I need to revisit this point right here and right now—this point where the pivotal light done come on! You didn't want me to get here, Satan! But I'm HERE NOW—HALLELUJAH!

So, let me calm down.

You Too!

You feel like you're to blame for what you're going through? This may be so, but guess what. After you repent, the stuff I wrote above APPLIES TO YOU TOO! You can make your altar here, where God's wanted you to come running to Him for correction, instruction, and deliverance from guilt and condemnation. You too are His creation in whom He wrought purpose, value, and ASSIGNMENT. Do NOT get bogged down with a rut type of mentality any longer. Confess, ask for forgiveness, and be FREE and dangerously obedient to the Father of Lights and the God of Wonders, one of which YOU ARE!

Whew! How do I close this piece?

Wanna' know where you are? You're in the perfect moment to push ahead into the purposes and plans God has for you, thus the purposes and plans He has for others whom you encounter on a daily basis, or have not met heretofore. You've got God stuff to do. And your effectiveness hinges on your awareness of your freedom. Get acquainted with the fact that God has a strange way of liberating us (ask Jesus). The deeper we go in Him, the more costly the trip.

Oct 6, 2018 — **Entry 12** — 4 min read

Trivial Pursuit Puts on Reckless Abandon

There's an old milk commercial that shows a scrawny little kid holding a carton of milk, looking in a mirror talking to himself about how, with his body, no girl's gonna' go for him. As the kid talks, his reflection talks back to him while drinking the milk, aging, and physically maturing. By the end of the commercial, the reflection staring back at him is his handsome, muscular, high school senior self who stands with a pretty girl on his arm. He drinks his milk with mild confidence and ease, causing his young, scrawny version to rapidly drive the milk carton up to his mouth in great anticipation of getting to his senior year in high school.

Runt of the Litter? NOT!

I remember hitting a certain age when I didn't appreciate being the little one of the bunch, as I was smaller than many of my peers (and still am). I certainly felt like the majority of my friends towered over me and possessed bigger hips and back sides. I just knew they were getting more looks from boys than I was, and I sometimes yielded to feeling less significant than girls who were larger in physical presence. However, 20+ years later, it trips me out that what I thought mattered so much back then is far from carrying the same weight now. It's even crazier that trading the right counsel for the wrong counsel can cause one to totally miss the mark on how to view oneself. And when it comes to facing an enemy—hmph! You BEST know who you are. If you don't, *YOU GON LEARN TUH-DAY!*

God Moves Us

The Bible talks about how, when the children of Israel left Egypt and Pharoah's evil, grueling treatment, the Egyptians pursued them to the Red Sea. Israel began to fear they'd left Egypt only to die in the wilderness, to which God had led them. However, Moses told them to 1.) not be afraid, 2.) be firm, confident, and unphased by their enemies, and 3.) watch God save them from the thorn in their side, AKA the hateful Egyptians. Moses went on to say, "Those Egyptians whom you have seen today, you will never see again. The LORD will fight for you while you [only need to] keep silent and remain calm" (Exodus 14:13, 14).

As I was driving home today, I realized that the *driving* away of an enemy is not always because it chooses to retreat, but because God moves *us* to new levels of maturity and restful confidence, which wash the enemy out, drowning it in the tide of our knowledge of who we are in Him. We arrive at a resolve that shifts our focus from enemy to Master and Father, who's equipped us with all we need to conquer ANY naysayer. Thus, the way we see a threat becomes totally revolutionized, and we no longer fear whom or what once taunted us—they've become way smaller in comparison to the ocular hold we have on our God.

It works the same way when we fast, turning away food for a time so God can move us out of our spiritual lethargy and cause us to ascend to higher heights in the way we receive Him. Our discernment clears, and our reception of spiritual things becomes smooth flowing—more effortless. We rise to a richer spiritual altitude.

Trivial Pursuit?

I think we also see this in our prayer lives. When we ask God to give us the desires of our hearts (Psalm 37:4), our intent lies in the level of our pursuit of Him. This verse first instructs the believer to be delighted by God—to find enjoyment in knowing Him—to be attracted to all things Him. This leaves us wanting what He wants—regardless—and we want Him to put in our hearts the desires *He* wants there. When we treat Him like He's Santa Claus, we ask Him to give us what *we* want.

Pastor Bill Johnson of Bethel Church says that if God's not talking to us, we need to talk to Him about what *He* cares about. Pastor Johnson also says that if we don't come out of prayer with our faith renewed, then all we're doing is complaining [and I'll add that we're running down a laundry list of requests that might not mean a hill of beans to Him].

Reckless Abandon

There's a reckless abandonment with which the mature Christian lives. Those who are close to God step further and further away from themselves as they swoon for Him and His heart—*His* mind about things. Our perpetual goal is to keep the line of communication open on our end so that we're never foreign in His presence—that our communion with Him is (as my pastor says) one seamless garment of prayer, praise, and worship.

There's an awesome sense of security that we have when the intense interests of our hearts are the intense interests of God's. We can't go wrong panting for God and all He desires. With this posture, we'll always look up and find ourselves in the right place in life, being and doing as God would have it.

Oct 9, 2018 — **Entry 13** — 4 min read

You Best Believe!

So, there's this episode of *Mike and Molly* where Molly, who's a school teacher on the show, is talking to her students about going after their dreams. In the middle of her speech, as she comically tells them their futures hinge on the state standardized test they're about to take, her mind begins spiraling, and she realizes the feeling of suffocation caused by her daily grind as she quickly processes that she's not doing what she dreamed of doing. She then tells the kids that she's going to pursue her dreams as she casually meanders to the classroom window and jumps right out of it. She's later found (by her police officer husband, Mike, who happens to be cruising in his squad car) walking down the street in the pouring rain! I died laughing inside thinking, *This is exactly what I feel to do most days from room 213 in my school building.*

An Urban Cry

I was even telling my students today about my frequent desire to escape the things I encounter, daily, as an educator in an urban high school. I was telling them this from the standpoint of the critical nature of their choices within the school day. However, the conversation quickly transcended what they do in the school building to what goes on in their lives *outside* of school.

For example, they know I'm allergic to profanity. When they let 'er rip, I tell them to stop cursing because I break out in hives at the profane things that leave their mouths. They get a chuckle out of it—especially because of my delivery—but it really rings true in my heart that there's another way of expression besides the one that comes so naturally to them.

So, today, several shouting matches ensued between students during my plea of exasperation, which was brought on by the fact that 85% of my 4th period casually entered the classroom LATE, postponing the lesson I'd prepared by 10-15 minutes. Why so long a postponement? Because of the way that many of them enter a room—loudly and insensitive to the environment that's already been set.

This Is How We Do It, Mrs. Payne!

During one of the shouting matches between two students—one, who was in support of my stance and the other, who had some opposing views—profanity went flying between them. When I addressed the profanity and encouraged them to hash things out void of using this type of language, one of them said, "My bad, Mrs. Payne. But you ain't gonna' get nuthin' across by speakin' nice to people. You gotta' cuss at 'em." My reply to that was, "That's really unfortunate that things are like that for you guys."

When I asked another student why this is "the way" to communicate, she said it's because she was brought up like this. To second this, I've seen text messages—from several different parents to their children—with profanity in them (probably not a shocker to you). And the focus of this piece is not profanity but the belief by my students that there's no other way to live. This is it for them—the cussing, the sexual perversion, the grade levels behind in their skill sets, the paycheck-to-paycheck and government assistance style of living.

How Can I Pray?

When I offered for any and every one of them to let me know what I can pray for (considering they know I'm a believer, having me last year as 9th graders), two of them said they would give me an answer later. So, I'll keep praying for them ALL but will use my cheat sheet for the two who give me specifics of what to pray about (when they get back to me).

These students are products of environments where talk about prayer or God or hope or faith seems minimal to nonexistent. These staples of the Christian faith are not *normal* to them because they're of the world, which is why they look at me like I've just told them the strangest thing ever when I continually challenge them on their choices, telling them there's a better, life-giving way. Seemingly everything dirty, and sinful, and dark, and lustful is their norm. And this ... just ... CAN'T ... go on. This isn't only from a teacher's standpoint for the sake of relief in the classroom, but it's from a believer's perspective, knowing the reality of their present and future condition/destination if they and their families don't hear and receive the TRUTH.

The Bible says, "Enter through the narrow gate. For wide is the gate and broad is the road that leads to destruction, and many enter through it. But small is the gate and narrow the road that leads to life, and only a few find it" (Matthew 7:13-14).

PRAYER Is the Rule of the Day!

I can tell you this. Prayer and intercession are the appetizer, the main course, *and* the dessert in this here time of my life—and they forever shall be. For my students, for their families, and in all things, I've committed to pray because I don't have a definite understanding of how long I'll be a school teacher, but I **guarantee** I'm pulling some souls up with me. Somebody's gonna' be changed because they know me, and—be it while I'm still in the school or after I'm gone—will want to know my **GOD**. If I'm going through the anguish, the tears, the feeling of suffocation, and the fight, oh—you BEST believe there are spoils of war that'll come from this.

You **BEST** believe it.

Oct 13, 2018 — *Entry 14* — 4 min read

Cornered and Better for It

I wonder how many people around you are ready to scream or burst at the seams. How many of them are on the verge of quitting? How many of them are suffering or struggling with something? How many egg shells do we walk on every day out of familiarity with being UNfamiliar with folks? To how many people do we avoid saying something that could provide another option or present another way of thinking? How many opportunities for candor do we extinguish for fear of laughter, weird stares, or judgment?

Cornered

I've been pushed—cornered—by God in this time of my life, and from it comes a walk and conversation that's fueled by no longer caring about how I'm received. It's like the whole Clark Kent-phone booth yields Superman type of thing, but not really, considering that I'm being changed while living and moving with the pace of life in which I've been graced to flow. I've not been tucked away in a four-corner hide-out or closed in from society (though many times I've wanted to be). Life has kept right on moving for me as it has for everyone else.

A few years ago, my world, as I knew it, actually spun out of control, through what I perceived as a demonic attack on my mind, exposing me to a whole new level of warfare. And I've learned, like I've never known before, to depend on God and what HE says about me. The attack quickly showed me I was no longer Mrs. IN CHARGE like I foolishly thought I was, as I was stripped down to focusing on the basics of my Christian walk—taken back to my ABCs of faith. Yes (and quite honestly), prior to that point, I'd depended on and believed God. I'd been plugged into Him and was doing what I knew to keep things simple and obey Him. However, through this warfare, He's shown me a deeper level of trust in Him, revelation of who He is, and knowledge of the weight His voice ***better*** carry in my life (YOU HEAR ME?!?!).

The Onslaught

All I know to say about the onset of this perceived attack is that it came out of nowhere. One moment I was watching a movie at home with my son, and the next I was doing my best to fight off a barrage of horrible, fear-fueled thoughts, coming one after the other, in full onslaught mode. These thoughts carried the assignment of destroying my confidence in who God says I am, the quality mother I have the right and grace to be, and the bodacious babe of a wife He's equipped me to walk as. Within moments of this onslaught, I was in mental and emotional turmoil that had bewilderment and anxiety running rampant within me—playing laser tag. The walls of my mind and heart were being torched by fiery darts, and I thought, *What, in TARNATION, is going on here?!?!*

Pages Out of Job

It has recently come out of my pastor's sermons that there's been some formidable warfare (which is Job-like in origin) happening in the lives of believers in this season. Just like it happened to Job in the Bible, there's been some spirit realm conversation about some of us, indicating God's confidence in our faithfulness to Him through WHATEVER. So, that hedge you felt lift from around you, letting some assigned attacks through ... check in with God about this. He might show you the AFFIRMATIVE He gave the kingdom of darkness to "try if they want to" with you.

Amazingly, through this season of warfare (not that I should've expected anything less), God's calmly and passionately pursued me with His wisdom, His Word, and His presence. He's been right there at every turn encouraging me, telling me, over and over again, that I am who He says I am. He's been taking my resolve in His nature and ability, and is developing more beastly roots within me. I'm sure Satan hoped against the TURN UP this has brought outta me! I mean, realistically he should've just left me alone because he done barked up the wrong tree with this one, and done unleashed a level in me that's pushing me to do my part in piercing his darkness.

Backfire

He's already seeing the oil drip from this pen as I write. He's seeing these messages speak to people who are going through [or have gone through] similar things, either having not been vocal about it or wondering if they're all alone. He's seeing the decimation of the believed lie that a believer's life is void of trouble (shoot—sometimes it feels like a messy one on steroids). He hates that hopeless people are seeing the key difference between the life of a believer and that of a non-believer as trouble with Christ versus trouble without Him. And they're choosing life with Him, finding that "yet holding onto Him" will put them in a place of eternal rest versus eternal torment. Thank You, Jesus!

So, I inquire—

What can compare to the position I hold in God's heart? What's worth more than knowing Him? Who or what could ever replace this God? And who or what has the audacity to try this in my life?

Nothing! No one! Game over! Deal done! Rules broken! Possibilities endless! Suuuuuu-weet victory!

Oct 20, 2018 — *Entry 15* — 5 min read

Who's Parenting Whom?

Chile, parenting–

Ever felt or caved under the perceived pressure of other people watching while you parent? And don't let it be a tense moment when your child or the children you have charge over act out or display less than desired behavior. You've felt those watchful eyes burning a hole in the back of your neck or the side of your face saying, "Oh! You BETTA do somethin!" haven't you?

Well, these days, being candid and bare before God, in all things, helps me not to cave under the unspoken expectations of others when it comes to the way I parent. I know I need God's help in everything else, so why not ask Him for help with parenting too? I mean, He is the ultimate parent. What sense does it make to avoid His advice about what to do with these peeps He's given us charge over? And then here's another thing–asking for help from others is wise too. Our boys run into behavior bumps here and there, and hubby and I have been leaning on our family members and trusted friends to lend a hand in advice, correction, encouragement, and just that love stuff. Shoot! We appreciate and are grateful for this communal lift in building our boys, ensuring they develop as God would have it.

I mean, sometimes I don't *feel* like parenting (throwing stones, are we?).

Do you ever think about God not feeling like repeating what He already told you? Or that He just doesn't feel like explaining some things to you? I thought about this when my son asked me to explain something to him while we rode in the car the other day. He didn't ask me anything complicated. It was something that required me to explain a couple of steps to him that I just didn't feel like exerting the mental energy to do.

Come Again?

My new homie, Sarah Jakes Roberts, who's becoming one of my favorites to hear speak, spoke a message called *God Listened.* In her message, she talked about God–when we request that He "come again"–responding to our prayers. She referenced how people who are hard of hearing may ask you to "come again" when you're talking to them and they don't understand what you've said (I remember this as a southern girl growing up in Texas). Pastor Jakes Roberts got to a moment in her message where she said that sometimes, God won't "come again" because you done already heard Him say what He said–several times. He done obliged you and done "come again" repeatedly.

Whut'Cha Ask Fuh It Fuh!?!?

In the same vein, Rickey Smiley did a stand-up comedy routine where he talked about his grandmother who would, when he was young, get mad when her grandkids asked for food but didn't eat it. He specifically talked about asking her for a banana once, and she gave him a way-past-ripe one. You know the one I'm talkin' about—the one that's barely holding on to its peel—the black one you can smash just by looking at. That one! Well, after seeing it, he told her he didn't want it, and she roared back, "Well whut'cha ask fuh it fuh!?!?" in that southern black grandmama type of way!

God Be Like ...

You think it may be the same way with God? We ask Him for something, and when He gives it to us, we forget about how hungry we were at the times of request. We hit moments when we no longer want what He's given us—correct? I really do wonder if God rolls His eyes at this kind of stuff.

So, in the times that my children require mothering when I don't feel like it, or the times when I want to jump off the School Teacher Train before it's time, or the times when I internally (and externally) roll my eyes at the husband I fell head over heels in love with in my 20s, I think back on just how thirsty I was for these people and opportunities before God blessed me with them. There's the process of having the babies (after miscarrying one and falling down the stairs with another in the womb—which happens to be the younger boy who's elation I can currently hear in the other room as I type this at the chiropractor's office). Then there's the job that, almost 15 years ago, was essentially handed to me—the one I *didn't* have to interview for. There's also the courtship (with Kwesi) that God looked after. And there are those who love us, who chose to walk with and hold us accountable. I'm reminded to appreciate God for what He's given me—what I've asked for.

Fuh Real-Fuh Real?

Here's a twist though. What about when we question God, asking Him to "come again" after we've heard something from Him that we're not sure is really Him or just our own desires? You know what I'm talking about? What about when He says something we actually *like* to hear? Something we didn't even initiate?

About six months ago, I started to hear some things about the next chapter for my family and me that put excitement in the air of my world. I went back to God several times asking, "God, really?" I started to pull on some ladies whose prayer lives I respect, asking them to pray around what I was hearing so that I had some accountability and didn't just run with what I heard because it sounded favorable to me. And what did God do? He kept pouring and pouring what He was saying into me. It seemed He didn't mind "coming again," but I believe this is because of my heart posture. I've hit a space, where regardless of the counsel, I *really* want to be obedient. So, I don't want to even get remotely comfortable with just an idea or wish that I have—calling it God. I'd rather hear the truth and get comfy with *that.* This way I don't have to get over hurt feelings and deep disappointment after learning God never said what I said He said.

Facts

God parents from a seat of stability. He makes decisions based on His infinite, Fatherly wisdom. He loves us and gives us what He knows will teach us the lessons we need in order to reflect His person-hood. He does this so we can shine as the beams of light He crafted us to be to this world. I can't afford to diminish my shine by trying to be the parent when I'm the child.

Oct 22, 2018 — *Entry 16* — 3 min read

God, You Are Hot Sauce

In September this year, I started getting up at 4 a.m. on work days to ensure that I spend time in my Word before work. My time is four o'clock because the gym opens at five, and Kwesi and I have mapped out a schedule around who will go to the gym on what morning.

A couple of Sunday mornings ago, I rose earlier than normal (I think because my body has adjusted to the earlier rising these days). I pulled my devotional books and Bible off the floor by my side of the bed, and when I got ready to crack them open, Kwesi had rolled over, and he began to pray what sounded like, "God, You are hot sauce."

He's Leading!!!

What he really said was, "God, You are our source" in a groggy Trinidadian line of thanksgiving first thing in the morning. But even when I thought he was calling God a spicy topping, I was grateful to go with him in prayer because my husband was leading me in PRAYER! He was LEADING me to time with God, and you betta' know I was gonna' stick around to hear the connection between our God and this kickin' condiment!

The bottom line I'm drawing here is gratefulness that the leader of my home—MY leader—chose to lead me in this moment. So, I briskly pushed aside the qualms I was about to have regarding his decision to pray during *my* personal time with God. See, quite often (because of the task-oriented person I am) I can miss what God wants to do—the sincerity of a moment and the authenticity of a lesson—due to being caught up in a routine (thankfully, I'm learning to relax and grow these days).

The Forward Lean

That morning, Kwesi also prayed, "God, help us keep You on the forefront of our minds." This gave me the visual of a person either leaning forward or backward, based on his thinking. In this illustration, a person tilts forward if he leans into the present or future through his thinking. The inverse of this forward-leaning person is one being weighted backward if he always has the past on his mind. I want to be a person leaning to the front (the way that some at my church say our pastor walks with the utmost briskness—ahaaaaaaaaa!).

How's Your Wave Game?

I don't want the state I'm in to mean something negative for those connected to me. The story of Jonah causes me to think about this in "waves," for I wonder if anybody else on any other boat in the same stormy sea as Jonah, was rocked the same way he and the crew he endangered were rocked. This makes me think, *When I'm having a crappy day, does my family suffer? When I'm frazzled and angry, do my man and kids have to inhale the second-hand smoke from it?* This is a chin check for sure.

My forward-leaning pastor often says that a mature Christian has good and bad days but stays even keel through them both. This is not an expectation that one isn't honest about what he experiences, but it does mean that one stays white-on-rice close to the posture of **God's got me, regardless—on the hill *and* in the valley.** This helps me to do my darndest to "know how to get along and live humbly [in difficult times], and ... also know how to enjoy abundance and live in prosperity. In any and every circumstance I [want to] have learned the secret [of facing life], whether well-fed or going hungry, whether having an abundance or being in need" (Philippians 4:12 AMP).

The Apostle Paul put the smack down right there for us in that verse, showing us that the grand scheme of the Christian life strips us from letting our emotions lead. In this dance, we ought to have heavy heart convictions that steer our ships (lives) always in the direction in which God leads. So, I leave you with a quote from Pastor Bill Johnson of Bethel Church.

"The mind is a better student than teacher, a better follower than leader. It's to be taught by the spirit—not to rule over and dominate the Christian life. The renewed mind considers reality from what the Lamb (Jesus) has accomplished. Therefore, all [believers] come under the redemptive work of Jesus. [This redemptive work is] done on the believer's behalf, and this is the normal life for [said] believer."

I don't want the world's normal. I'll take the normal Pastor Johnson is talking about.

Get Outta' My Face, Rat Race!

You ever rolled your eyes at time constraints? What does it mean when they annoy you?

Ever awakened wondering what day it is, only to realize it's a non-work day, which makes you OH SO THANKFUL?

Have you, at this realization, mentally and emotionally thrown up your hands—thanking God you don't have to part with your pillow to hit the morning grind as hard as you normally do?

As Christian radio host Willie Moore Jr. says, it just makes you feel good in your SHAH-NAH-NAH!

Just last Saturday morning, I had this experience as my alarm went off! I felt so relieved that I didn't have to bid my current state of stillness and quiet goodbye. I got to stay right where I was, betwixt my warm bed sheets, inside my home, separated from the brisk morning elements just on the other side of the wall beside my bed. Oh, what a wonderful moment!

What to Do?

So, what are we to do when we must leave a safe, cozy environment only to thrust ourselves into the rat-race-feel of life?

Welp, the trick is carrying that internal stillness into our day as the gears begin to grind. And actually, this is not a trick, but it's a settling in our hearts that God's in and with us; therefore, we're fine, regardless. This posture of rest, of course, is for the believer. And not to throw shade or cast stones at the non-believer, but I cannot avoid shining a light on the factual truth that Christ followers are saved from more than just an abysmal, hell-fire-after-death experience. We're saved from an on-earth, mark-missing detriment of life withOUT Christ. We're called to be ALL JESUS EVERYTHING.

I know this may sound like TOO MUCH, but the reality is that as the believer continues to live, our lives should increasingly be magnetically drawn, by the Holy Spirit within us, toward the righteousness that IS God. Everything in our lives should revolve around obedience to Him. Additionally, and amazingly, He speaks to us—backed by His written Word—in order that we consistently perceive Him as He provides His spot-on, specific instruction.

Here's where the intimacy that blows a mind happens. Our Father finds us right where we are, addressing everything that involves us AND OTHERS. He, as we begin to see maturely, talks to us the way He does and allows us to go through the things we go through for the sake of soooooooo many besides ourselves. We're to be letters "that anyone can read by" observing us. Christ writes them (the believers being the letters) "—not with ink, but with God's living Spirit; not chiseled into stone, but carved into human lives" (2 Corinthians 2:13 AMP).

More Than a Come-to-Jesus Moment

This is how we evangelize, living lives that are unavoidably convincing of the downright necessity of CHRIST in the heart. As people encounter us, their insides should cry out for the internal rest and peace they sense we obtain. And a quite liberating concept that's recently been highlighted at my church by my pastor is that evangelism is not to only be directed at the individual with*out* Christ. Believers need to be evangelized as well. We need encouraging reminders of the undeniable requirement that a soul has for oneness with Christ—that we may keep trudging, keep fighting, keep being faithful, and keep being hopeful in the very thing that attracted us to Jesus in the first place.

When we begin to yield to our humanity, inching closer toward the illusion that Christ is okay with playing the role of supplement in our lives, a brother or sister evangelist comes along to remind us to rearrange our priority list, pushing prayer and meditating on the Bible back to their proper places. Bro and sis come to sharpen us again, telling us that things are not only about us, but that they're about our obedience to God in His grand scheme. Thus, we're recharged and not allowed to regress in our growth or occupy complacency. So, don't get mad when you're chin checked (one of my increasingly favorite terms) by another believer. It's what God requires of them. If they left you dull, they'd be doing you a disservice.

Francis Chan put it like this:

"The point of your life is to point to Him. Whatever you are doing, God wants to be glorified, because this whole thing is His."

Your life, believer or not, is not your own. You're not the author, nor are you the controller. This realization often readjusts my vision, making me see that much of the pressure in my day is self-created. Heck yeah, I still have stuff to do—a Kingdom family to help weaponize and lead, a local ministry in which to serve with a pure heart, and broken students to pull up from the pits in which they blindly dwell. However, because my primary call is showing people JESUS, all of the things that make up my daily grind shouldn't be allowed to make me anxiety-ridden or uncontrollably annoyed. So, when the wrong emotional state begins to increase within, it's my hope that my ALL JESUS EVERYTHING posture leads me to quick remembrance that I've really got nothing to be up in arms about. My posture—regardless of my external pace—is one of peaceful "Get outta my face, rat race" rest that laughs at whatever tries to make me forget the heavenly place with Christ in which I'm seated. Geoffrey Golden speaks so well of this place at the front of his song "Glory to the Lamb." Search for it and listen.

Nov 4, 2018 — **Entry 18** — *4 min read*

Humble Pie Is Filling

I'm a patient—

And I'm one for so many reasons—

I'm a cancer patient because it's only the blood of Jesus that's made it possible for me to have the Holy Spirit—who gives me the strength to shun the very appearance of cancerous evil—within. I'm a mental health and heart patient because it's only the Lord who has done things for me which have penetrated my heart in such a way that I cannot deny who He is and what He does. This provides much needed guidance for my mind, which is a better follower than leader. It needs to closely follow after a heart that's been changed and is faithfully held by an almighty God such as mine. I'm, in essence, a surgical patient because I have a life-long stay in my Father's Holistic Health Surgical Center. I'm always in need of His touch, and I pray I'll never again walk under the falsehood that I'm in control.

I Need Help—I Need God

I've hit the cusp of understanding that needing help is not a shameful place. It's human, honest, and is, quite frankly, the place where the devil cringes—watching people discover their need for God. Matthew 5:3 says, "Blessed are the poor in spirit, for theirs is the Kingdom of Heaven." This means that we are in a blessed place to know and admit to the evident God-sized void in our lives. We're fortunate when we understand that being at the end of our rope is "where it's at" because this is the inception of our pining for a ridiculously capable God who knows exactly what we need, exactly how to fix, exactly what to say, exactly how to hold, exactly how to chasten, and exactly where to lead.

His grace finds us and continues to perpetuate our understanding of His present and active nature as God. This understanding explodes into an awesome zeal that makes us pant for more interaction with Him. We become increasingly aware that He's waiting for us to take required steps of obedience right into His volcanic love that ransacks our self-created customs, which we foolishly thought would work for every season.

A Lesson in Crunches and Clothes

Yesterday, I was at the gym doing crunches, and as I counted from one to 25, I began to think about each year of my life—from birth to 25 years old. I began to, with each count, evaluate whether I've gotten better or worse each year—whether I've, overall, grown spiritually weaker or stronger as I've aged. I thank GOD for my realization that [after 25 plus 13 more years], I've gotten better and not worse! I've gotten collectively stronger and not weaker!!! Wiser and not more foolish!!! THANK YOU, JESUS! And come to think of it, this mentality helped me do my crunches to fidelity, as I had the drive to, with each crunch, be stronger and go harder on the next. This life journey has delivered some great lessons to me, one of which is the critical nature of my required vulnerability with God. I don't know what the foolish attraction to try and save face before Him is about, but it's just that—foolish and a waste of time.

At some point after I got home from the gym, I was bringing some of our cubs' clothes downstairs to put in the wash, and Kwesi asked me, "Are those regular dirty or urinated-upon dirty?" I literally laughed out loud at this candid question from a father of two boys, one seven, the other three [because I knew exactly where he was coming from]! But as I continued on to the basement, where the washer and dryer are, I thought about how people unfairly categorize the dirt in others' lives, putting some dirt in the *Excusable* box and other dirt in the *Inexcusable* box. We call some stuff "regular dirty" and other stuff "urinated-upon dirty".

Even doing this with our own dirt, we view some things we do or think as just a little sprinkle of dirt that we don't need to feel that badly about. However, there are some other things we've done, said, or thought that we don't want many to know about. Here's the thing, however. Sin is sin to God. Dirt is dirt to Him. If somethin' ain't right, according to His holy standard, He doesn't require our repentance for the part we thought was crossing the line; He requires our repentance for it all. And He's not surprised or caught off guard by our faults. Shoot! There are even some challenges, some seasons He allows because He wants to see if we're going to be humble enough to ask

Him or someone for help. Through this, He shows us that He's the only one suited to carry a God complex. He wants us to see that His responsibilities are too heavy for our shoulders, but our weight, He can most certainly bear—and that quite effortlessly. He's God ALONE for countless reasons. Let Him be that for you.

Nov 23, 2018 **Entry 19** *4 min read*

Held

"The deliverance starts when we are no longer impressed by the size of our problem [because that is when we don't fear]." - Pastor Bill Johnson (words in brackets are mine)

God-inspired afterthought–

"As we are not to be impressed with the problem or the size of it, it speaks to where we walk when we remain level headed after seeing that the enemy has fled. For, when we understand our divine authority, we are more aware of the fact that evil is SUPPOSED to be the intimidated party–not us."

- Scripture reference Psalm 3

"And the Lord is saying, 'Let ME be who I AM for you.' "

I Still Agree

The above quote is a Facebook post of mine from almost exactly two years ago. The thing I'm consistently able to say as I repost old posts is, **"I STILL AGREE!"** This never fails, and the reason why this is so impressive—even relieving—to me is that there can be many ups and downs in a day—let alone within the span of a year. The way I feel right now may not be the way I feel an hour from now, and I'm able to say that I still agree with things I've posted years ago? This makes me smile, especially because these have been words of substance. To be able to still stand in agreement with them is a mark of consistency.

This is certainly not a "toot toot" of my own horn, but a reflective praise to God for keeping me. He has shown me what being at the end of my rope means—greater trust in Him, leading to higher spiritual heights/deeper spiritual depths—whichever way you want to see it.

People and Prayer in the Process

To think about where my head has been at some moments and on some days, I'm in amazement of God's keeping fortitude. I'm truly grateful that He's continuing to help me appreciate PROCESS—and the messy kind, to boot! Yes, the highs are mixed in with the lows, but I think my bottom line here is that I want both my highs and lows to be overly familiar with my God and His reach to me through love and support of others. One of these "others" is my husband who's such an impressive sounding board for me. He's proven—since our before-marriage days—that I can share anything with him, and he'll handle my words with a cool-ness that reassures he's not going anywhere just because things aren't stellar or going the way we may falsely think they should go.

I was chatting with some close girlfriends of mine, and we were talking about challenges we have. I shared with them that what's beautifully amazing, in all that we as women go through, is God's faithfulness throughout our experiences (the whole gambit). Additionally, and wonderfully refreshing, God doesn't require that we mask our struggle but that we acknowledge what it is and not feel spiritually lesser when we need to be aided or uplifted by community. I believe He's pleased when His people are candid and humble, for this is what He models for us through Jesus. We're better for the pain, the challenges, and the struggle if we're open to receiving help through them. From here, we might gain a testimony of navigation that will pick somebody else up and encourage them on their path.

Also, in this season where prayer has taken a different face and has put on a cape in my life, I'm finding that this privilege afforded to me is certainly more than a tic on a to-do list, something I can tell others I'll do for them, or a Christian pastime to keep me off the hell-bound train. It's an access point that requires my way of life to relax its shoulders, fasten its grip around this metaphorical machete, and get tuh slicin', clearing the air and stirring up trouble at the same time. So, my choice to pray reflects a heart willing to let God lead—in all things.

Narrow My Focus

Another thing that recent life is teaching me is to narrow my focus and do what I can to cut down on the crazy. The other day, I was at the gym doing crunches and noticed, on the TV screen in front of me, that the gym afforded me the luxury of knowing what was showing on six channels all at the same time (all on one TV). NAW! UHN UHN! This was *not* a luxury for me because I had too many options—too many things to try and keep up with at once. Sensory OVERLOAD was my short-lived experience with that TV before I decided to turn away from it. Give me one channel, please and thank you —just one.

This need transfers over to the space in which God is doing something tremendous in me. As I was telling one of my close girlfriends recently, I don't know how this process in me is **looking**, but it sure **feels** messy sometimes. However, God started it—and I know He's gonna' bring me to a tipping point where glorious benefits will run over my brim and bless the socks off of many (these socks-off blessings have already begun, actually).

As I've written in other pieces, my perpetual prayer is, "Lord, keep me most aware of You at all times." In the midst of being a wife, a mom, a school teacher, and one beggar who shows other beggars where I've found bread, God needs to be my focal point. Away with busying myself to know what's showing on the other channels. I stay sane as I keep my heart attuned and my eyes glued to the God channel. For on His channel are all of the reminders of how to gracefully navigate through my responsibilities.

God-Kissed Little Girl

I hit these increasing God-kissed moments when I look forward to casting my cares on Him. I remember that I'm His little girl and that I've got a BIG DAD who wants me to always know that His capability to save, keep, comfort, and handle the responsibility of being my DAD is unceasing and un-toppable. Nobody's better at it than He is.

I love you, GOD.

*Natalie Grant's song "Held" came to mind as I ended this piece. Search it out and take a listen.

Dec 15, 2018 — *Entry 20* — 6 min read

New Wine

It all came together for me last Sunday as Mr. Blanding prayed. He was a man on holy fire when all of the congregation gathered around the altar for prayer. To hear a man pray to God like he did ... crying out with no shame and with an earnestness that let me know I was truly in the right place. Physically, I was covered by my husband, whose hand rested on my shoulder, as I knelt with our three-year-old on my lap. We sat to the left of our seven-year-old, who knelt with his father's right hand on his shoulder. This was our family—right there at the altar. Paint a picture? Good. It's the right one.

All on the Altar

We, along with other families and members of our church, came to the altar and prayed to God under the leadership of this seasoned Mr. Blanding. His wife, Mrs. Deborah (one of my favorite ladies), stood beside him as he prayed fervently for God's covering over our young people. He also steered us through repentance for negligence to obey God at turns in our relationships with Him. The way this man climbed the steps to the stage, fell to his knees, curled up on the floor, and led us directly to God's throne in humility created a powerfully fueled moment.

He roared with such a desperate cry in praise to the Lord toward the end of the prayer—a roar that erupted like a volcano, bursting with lava, which caught the souls of us around the altar. Seeing the head of a household, a man with age behind him, a strong male presence, a manly man be freely vulnerable and unhindered in his worship of our strong God said to me, "Yeah, girl! You're in the right place, right now!"

The strength of this moment hangs with me days later as I think of its fanciful nature. It was like a dream to me—a woman who appreciates the structure that God instituted for the community and the family ages ago—falling under a godly man's leadership. To be covered by Pastor Lawrence, Mr. Blanding, and my faithful husband in that moment of prayer on God's altar was a place of comfort, requirement, and urgency all at the same time. To be held in the hand of God, led by strong godly men, and namely, walking through this phase of my life following my husband—who refuses to give up on finding God pleased with him as he leads our family—is an honor and a ride that won't quit.

Spirit Surfing

Then back to church last Tuesday for bible study. Deacon Montague prayed as a man in a moment when it was clear he knew he had God's attention and power at his disposal. I tell you, when a man will go hoarse for God, it says something about his core beliefs—which push him in leading a group of praying people to the Throne with the holy boldness we're afforded.

It was like we were Spirit surfing, holding Deacon Montague's coat tails as we rode deeper and deeper into the waves of God's glorious presence. We are a people who come to offer Him our praise and obedience regardless ***and*** because of all the factors in our lives.

Rights to Peace

This walk with God finds me in a place where I'm falling fast in love with hiding under the shadow of His wing—where I'm pleased to trust Him when it feels messy and unsettled—where there's an eerie freshness to signs of trouble, crushing, and groundbreaking. I'm in a place where, after a day filled with core-testing challenges, walking into my bedroom and seeing a made bed invites unexpected peace and spontaneously helps me feel just a tad better. This mimics what I believe is going on in the spirit realm. We believers are an abode that has rights to uninterrupted peace—a place where our rest is always a thing. This rest is ever present, residing in our peace-giving God, who, when we're most aware of Him, knocks our socks off with His serenity. This is a place of solitude, to which the most grand things in life pale in comparison. And this is a place of simplicity, where we're willing to *keep* things simple by leaving our hearts in the Master's hand—seeking to please Him with our obedience. These days, I'm realizing that obedience (and everything, really) starts in the heart (Prov. 4:23). So, herein lies the critical nature of one's core beliefs being where they should be—rooted in right relationship with God.

Chiropractic Recruitment

The other day, Asaiah (our three-year-old) was on the Chick Fil-a playground asking other kids if they've been to the chiropractor. When Asa, (our older son) stopped playing to tell me this, I thought his news would be about Asaiah asking kids if they knew Jesus. However, after thinking about it a bit, I was taken back to another piece I've written ("Get Back Right"), which is about an experience I had at the chiropractor's office and how it very closely mirrored being adjusted and fixed by God. So, the fact that Asaiah was recruiting other kids to the chiropractor tickled me because he was only modeling what we expose him to three times per week. This is encouraging, as it reveals what comes out of intention and consistency.

Don't Do It, Ms. Celie

Remember, in the movie *The Color Purple*, when Sophia sits at Mista's dining room table, right after Celie holds a knife to his throat? Sophia, who's been through some ground-breaking experiences herself, shares her story with others at the table. She, an African-American woman during segregation, tells of how her spicy temper won her the position of indentured servant to the mayor's wife, Mrs. Millie (Caucasian), who tried to bribe her for maid service one day in town by telling her that her little black children were "so clean." Sophia's choice words in declining Mrs. Millie's offer landed her in jail for a time (coupled with physical beating) and earned her years of service in the very place she, with much attitude, tried to avoid–Mrs. Millie's house. However, after serving her sentence and ending up back at home with family and friends (see the movie if you're lost here), Sophia, at Mista's table, slowly lets out a strangely mysterious, baritone chuckle at a time that doesn't seem appropriate (because a knife's just been held to a man's throat). She then abruptly cuts off her laugh with an impressive sharpness, drops her smile as she rocks back and forth, and begins to "school" Celie and all others at the table about decisions in life, starting with, *"Set up in that jail–"*

She tells of going through a process that taught her hard lessons of how to channel her voice, how to harness her strength and forthrightness, and how to finagle her way through a period in our country when racism, inequality, and segregation were extremely blatant and widely accepted. She opens some eyes around the table to what periods of crushing and pressing can teach a person. She exposes them to a sincere story of the newness that's come out of her pain and imprisonment to a situation she would have rather not known.

New Wine

I believe there is a sameness that links the holy fire, with which prayer has been going forth in my church recently, to crushing and pressing going on in the lives of the people in it. I believe life has been trying its best, lately, to wear us out. And what's surfacing is a holy determination to stay tight with JESUS! We keep gettin' squeezed and pressured over here, and what's oozing out is anointing that God is pleased to pour right on into these new wine skins. I am confident that I speak for many of us when I say the process ain't been pretty, but I believe that the glory coming from it will leave this crushing and pressing in the dust.

*Suggested song to search and listen to: "New Wine" by Hillsong Worship

Dec 26, 2018 — 3 min read

Entry 21

Snickerdoodle Love

Chile, this past Friday, I was released from school for Christmas break! I found myself at the opposite end of NOT knowing what to do with my time. I said to myself, "You gon' REST, chile."

True Hazard = No One Cares

That afternoon, I wound up sitting in my truck on the side of my street a few houses down from mine because on my way to get the truck's emissions tested, I decided that the chocolate candy bar and cup of milk I had brought with me deserved my full attention. So, in the jubilant Christmas-break-rest spirit, I pulled over and enjoyed my well-deserved snack without tasking myself with driving.

I turned on my hazards so people would know to go around me. But with this thought came another one, which reminded me that some years ago, I would've thought twice about flashing my hazards for such a frivolous thing as indulging in a chocolate candy bar—out of concern that somebody might actually think something was wrong and stop to help me. But NO—not in today's society. And ain't that a shame? Therefore, I put my hazards on with very little concern that someone would think something was wrong.

One of my very close friends was talking about something she needed to do, in her travels, that would require her to pull over on the side of the road. I told her that she should think twice about that because someone could think something was wrong [when it really wasn't] and stop to check on her. Her very quick and casual response to me was, "Girl, people don't care these days. Ain't nobody gonna' stop." When she told me this, I thought, *Man. That's not cool, but it's true.*

It's Just Right

Right about now, I bet you're wondering why this piece is titled the way it is. Well, when I think of a snickerdoodle cookie, I think of all that is right with sugar, flour, butter, cinnamon, and vanilla extract combined. There are a couple more ingredients belonging to this blessedly simple recipe, but what I'm saying here is the simplicity in making this deliciously scrumptious and comforting sweet is what makes it so great! You bite into a well-made snickerdoodle cookie, and tell me you don't like it. I'll then pray for you because apparently your God sensors are off, chile!

Loving others is equivalent to this simple sugary treat—it's just RIGHT. It's right to love. It's right to care about others. It's right to treat them as you want to be treated. It's right to show concern for them—to esteem them highly, understanding that the same God who made you made them too. When we live like this, we stick to treating people with truth at the core of everything we do.

As God has been showing me more about the importance and power in prayer, I'm seeing that it's not only a *good* thing to pray, but it's an *honor* to do it—not only for oneself but especially for others. For, with this perspective is the heart posture of wanting the same awesome impact of a God who fights for His people to happen in others' lives—that snickerdoodle love. It's just right.

The B-I-B-L-E

The Bible tells us that we should love others as we love ourselves *(Matt. 22:39)* and to even esteem others better than ourselves *(Phil. 2:3)*. It also tells us that we should always pray—about everything. Praying about everything runs in tandem with not being anxious or fearful about anything *(Phil. 4:6)*. And not submitting to fear speaks to our love walk—not only how we show love but how well we receive God's love for us *(1 John 4:8 & 18)*.

When a person has an issue with loving others, it's because he doesn't receive the love of God the right way. Therefore, he cannot properly give it. We gotta' receive God's good ole' snickerdoodle love, knowing that quality of life sure 'nuff depends on it.

Teddy P. almost had it right:

"Said now 70-30–
Now 60-40–
Talkin' bout a [snick-er-doodle] love, yeah"
(word in brackets is obviously mine and not Teddy's)

Jan 1, 2019 — **Entry 22** — *4 min read*

The Power of Purposeful Parenting

*(Jingle - **WINANS style!**)*
There's a new kinda' Cheerios
Waiting in your breakfast bowl
It's the honey of an 'O ...
It's Honey Nut Cheerios
It's the sunny taste of honey
Kinda' wholesome and kinda' nutty
It's a honey of an 'O ...
It's Honey Nut Cheerios!"

Now, what in tarnation (you may be thinking) do Cheerios have to do with anything? Welp, you know those people who turn a conversation about something as mundane as a bowl of cereal into being about God? The comedian Michael Junior does a bit [called *Are You Oversaved?*] on people like this. If you feel like it, pause right here, find it and watch. It will comically supplement this piece and is only two minutes and 21 seconds long.

A Parent's SUPERPOWER

Being *oversaved* may come across humorously, but there's something to the sincerity of a heart for God. The other day my boys dressed up in superhero costumes, performing as the superheroes they were dressed as. After they left the room, they came back and told me that I'm a super mom because I have kids who are superheroes. They even told me my superpower is kindness. I thought that was sweet. Plus, it parallels the design of parents passing things on to their kids through parenting, genetics, or observed behavior. I was oh so glad they found something positive to say that we have in common!

On the flip side, even when there are not-so-positive traits passed from parent to child, there's still a fix that can come from an Almighty God in heaven. When it seems that parents have done something on which a child's dysfunction can be blamed, this doesn't have to be the end-all-be-all.

The Bible points to the fact that God, being the original and ultimate Source, is consistent in His providence, and that even when father and mother fall short, the Lord comes through in the clutch to shift perspective and show us who's BOSS (Psalm 27:10). Because He's the end-all-be-all—shoot, He's ALL, period—nothing negative has to have the unconquerable power that causes one to live dysfunctionally for a lifetime. Additionally, nothing positive should overshadow the kind of overshadowing that God has the jurisdiction to do for any life.

I'm So Glad They Prayed

This Christmas, Kwesi, the cubs, and I went to be with my dad and stepmom in North Carolina, and we enjoyed ourselves very much. When we were getting ready to walk out of their front door to return home, Dad gathered us all to pray. This said to me that no matter that I'm a 38-year-old wife and mom, my godly and loving dad is still going to cover me out of his BIG love for me—the daughter he raised—and her immediate family of which she's now a part. Purposeful, godly parenting just can't be beat.

I can also recall when my mother and stepdad were about to depart from our Baltimore home a few years ago, to return to theirs in Texas; they prayed for us also. It was here, again, that I was reminded to be so grateful for godly parents—parents who, I'm sure, know they've not done all things right—but who love God and practice prayer. Being even more candid, it's been such a blessing to have step parents who have come right alongside my biological parents and have loved me as their very own. I'm talkin' bout a snickerdoodle kinda' love (see "Snickerdoodle Love" piece).

A Good Foundation

I remember, during moments of my childhood, perceiving that my mom was over-the-top with infusing Jesus in seemingly errrrryyyy-thang we did. Deuteronomy 11 gives me flashbacks when it says:

"Place these words on your hearts. Get them deep inside you. Tie them on your hands and foreheads as a reminder. Teach them to your children. Talk about them wherever you are, sitting at home or walking in the street; talk about them from the time you get up in the morning until you fall into bed at night" (vs. 18, 19 MSG).

I used to think, *Man! She can't* ***possibly*** *put a Jesus spin on* ***everything****! One day soon, she's gonna' run out of material!*

However, today I'm grateful these verses give me flashbacks to my childhood, for it was there, through purposeful parenting, that a foundation was established in me—a foundation that I live from today. I had a mama who didn't let no little teenage eye rollin' back her into a corner and cause her to let up on what she was dishin' out to me. As far as I remember, she remained consistent and added some spicy correction when I got too sassy about the way I received her God guidance. And I'm thankful for a father who showed me crazy love, as he would, on many school days, hand me the last few dollars he had in his wallet so I could eat lunch. He's a father who hung in there with me when I lost my natural mind at 15 years old and was making choices that he and God knew I hadn't been taught to make.

All JESUS Erryy-thang

So, when I laugh at the fact that some of the Winans siblings created a soulful rendition of the Cheerios jingle with a "Hallelujah" on the end of it, I'm laughing at myself because I now do stuff like that. I'll put a gospel typa' run on the end of a cartoon jingle I hear while watching something with my young sons simply because I'm a church girl. And I'm a church girl because my mama and daddy, though they parented me apart from each other for much of my life, had me in church errrrryyyyyy Sunday. From their labor of love—through introducing me to Christ—and keeping me involved in things Christ-centered, I'm more than wrapped up in JESUS today. And this, I know, will carry me through a life that's gotta' shine brighter as it goes on because the Bible says so (Prov. 4:18 NKJV).

Thank you, Mom and Dad, for being purposeful in your parenting. Because of you, all things are JESUS for me. Even Cheerios! Ha!

*Top this piece off by googling *Winans Honey Nut Cheerios Song.* Enjoy!

Feb 16, 2019 **Entry 23** *4 min read*

Cuz of God

Chile, I drove by a bridal shop the other day, saw the dresses in the front window, and gave the scene an eye roll.

Reason being? Yes, my wedding day was wonderful and blissful, but that's passed, now a milestone, and Kwesi and I, almost 13 years later, are on to things down the timeline in life. What I'm saying is we've progressed in seasons, and my appetite feasts upon being in whatever moment God has me. July 8th, 2006 was an altar experience that I won't forget, but even as I watch the video of it from time to time, as a reminder of what we founded our marriage upon, we're at deeper levels of life together now. You get me?

Another Lesson at the Chiropractor

It's like when I was at the chiropractor on the EMS table yesterday. One of the office attendants was speaking to a patient nearby, telling him of how she's gone back to school to become a PA. The patient showed excitement at the news and wished her luck in her endeavors. At that, I thought to myself that his wish of luck was a nice gesture, but it lacked a certain power—a type of support that could really do some damage to anything that would try to hinder her PA pursuits. I thought about how intercession is a much more worthwhile and qualifying resource to use to encourage and even cover others without saying any well wishes to them at all sometimes.

From my perspective as a believer, his good luck offering lacked the type of fervor that intercession for another carries. And this young man, I'm sure, was doing what he knew—saying what he knew to say—to encourage the next person, but it was like he had nothing else in his arsenal with which to boost her (if this makes sense). Not that, if he were a believer, he needed to drop everything, fall to his knees (pulling her to the floor with him) and go into some forced, deep, religiously strange ceremony to show her his support. All I'm saying is that in the moment, especially where I find myself concerning prayer and intercession, I just thought, *Man! There's a much more potent way to push her in her PA endeavor.*

Chile—That Fast

Just after the conclusion of a 40-day fast with my church, I find myself, by habit, still looking forward to the 4 a.m. prayer conference call, which started halfway through the fast but has now ended. I'm not confident I can articulate how surreal and heavenly those early morning prayer calls were. They facilitated enriching, empowering experiences, each morning, that felt like prophetic dreamlands—phone calls of connectivity with like-minded people who were just as desperate as I was (and still am) for proper movement toward God.

As the late Dr. Myles Munroe said in a sermon on fasting, one is almost afraid to break a fast, during which he has properly sought God, because he doesn't want to return to the old spiritual space he left. However, I'm thankful to God for moving me closer to Him during the fast. Shoot, yeah! I was hungry and frustrated sometimes when I couldn't eat (especially because I have small children who still required food in the midst of my fast), but it's even changed my after-fast eating habits. I find myself choosing more wisely, regarding what I put in my mouth and how much of it I consume.

Folks Need What We Have

And boy oh boy, the prophetic downloading (thanks, Pastor Lawrence) that God did before, during, and is continuing to do after the fast has been—BONKERS! My thirst for more of His voice, more of His messages, and more of His information continues and is greater. What has happened is that those of us who plugged into this time of consecration have heard God speak so much (and we believe He's telling the truth) that our heart postures and mindsets have become such that we walk about ready to be the encounters with Jesus that people need. We have been entrusted with too much understanding of who we are, how our Father sees us, and how desperately our spheres of influence need an encounter with Christ through us. Gospel singer Jonathan McReynolds tells us we're CHRIST REPRESENTERS.

Godspeed

So, I started this piece with an eye roll at a symbol of the sweet, God-centered, and surreal experience I established with the man of my life almost 13 years ago, only as an expression of understanding that God moves His people through life in seasons. Where I was (spiritually) years, even months, ago is not where you find me today. And it's not that I rush through life to get to the next spiritual altitude; it's that Godspeed is the believer's call to a readiness of self-abandonment for His pace. What He tells me to let go of, I want to let go of without whining. What He tells me about myself, I NEED to and WILL believe. And when He tells me to pray or intercede a certain way, I NEED to do just that (more about this coming in a future piece).

I cannot go back to the way things were (and they weren't bad at all). I've just gotta' go with God. That's all. And that's enough.

Feb 24, 2019 Entry 24 *5 min read*

Don't Renege on Your Release

Breathing hard between exercises, I answer the call by saying, "Hello."

Seeing that it's my son's school, I can only think of two things:

1. It's the nurse letting me know I need to pick him up early because something's wrong.

   OR

2. He's gotten into trouble.

It's the first reason, but only partially.

The nurse says (and it's not the regular nurse because I don't recognize the foreign accent on the other end of the call, and I figure Mrs. Worthington is out for the day), "Hello, Mrs. Payne. This is Such and Such from the school, and I have Asa here in the nurse's office with me."

I say, "Oh? What's going on? What symptoms is he experiencing?"

She replies, "He's complaining that his stomach hurts and that he's just not feeling well. I took his temperature and he does NOT have a fever. He ate his whole sandwich for lunch. He is complaining that he feels the need to throw up, but he has yet to do it. I really don't have much concern [but am calling you to err on the side of caution]"—*(words in brackets are my inference based on her tone of voice).*

I say, "Oh boy. Well, can you please do me a favor, ma'am?"

"Sure," she replies.

"Can you tell Asa that his mom says that maybe he should stay home tonight and not go to his friend's birthday sleepover since he's not feeling very well? Let me know how he responds, please."

Oh, YOU KNOW the response that comes back.

After taking a few seconds to offer my solution to Asa, she tells me, "He says he thinks he might start feeling better and that he's gonna' try and go back to class (she giggles)." She then adds, "Way to go, Mom!"

After a snicker, I say, "Please let him know I'll see him at PICK-UP TIME, and thanks for calling. You have a nice day!"

Gotta' say, I felt warm and tingly in that moment.

Tried the Okie Doke!

First of all, I had the day off because I took our four-year-old to his annual doctor's appointment, and I believe that because Asa knew this, he thought he could play around with my availability.

NOT SO!

Secondly, I was at the end of a workout at the gym, and that phone call broke my flow, with the potential to put me behind on the schedule I had going that day. Petty or naw?

Thirdly, I love the way the Holy Spirit works within His peeps. And because He's teaching me not to worry about the words I'll say, but to trust Him to give them to me at the proper times, beauty just masterfully flows out LIKE IT DID on this phone call! So, because his mama is lovin' this Holy Spirit thang, Asa had to go on 'head and internally fess up with the truth behind his actions. He thought he had me for the okie doke, but I called his bluff!

And yes! In this, I've picked up on a continued message God has begun talking to me about. He's saying if we're going to come on over into belief in something He says to us, we ought not go back to what we left. We have no need to return to former levels of faith or pull back on the confidence to which He's raised us. We have no real ground to renege on any baggage we've learned we can release.

No One Picks Me for Spades

I remember my college days when I was taught, by my college roommate and lifelong sister friend, LaShawn, that I'm not a very good spades player. I'd join spades games, thinking I was playing well with my partner, only to be told that I kept doing what's called RENEGING. You know what that is. It's when you play a card that's not the same suit of the card that leads when you actually have a card in your hand that can follow the leading suit. Yeah, well, I kept doing this. So, it's needless to say that since college, I'm happy to be a part of the social commentary around a spades game, but asked to pull up to the spades table for playing, I am not.

God has taken me through a season of giving Him my worries and fears, my anxieties and just old mental habits (which have no business with me anymore) of trying to control the past, present, and future—PRIDE, basically. He's taken me by the hand and has walked me through a type of wilderness where I've had to discover who I am all over again. He's shown me what my perception of Him should really be—just how aware of Him I should always want to be. And in my mind, He's been more than patient with me through all of my reneging while trying to get my posture right.

The Wilderness Done Made Me Dangerous

In this—though I've not been able to just pull away from the rest of society, from my family or other responsibilities, and am around people much of the time—I've felt quite alone while trying to learn the ropes in a place like this. But I'll tell you what—I've refused to give up on allowing God to simplify things, down to the least common denominator, for me. And I've learned to keep my hands open so I don't get comfortable with tightening my fingers around any single thing in my life. Nothing that I encounter—God's teaching me—should have the power to force me into a space where I'm not most aware of Him. For, when I'm most aware of Him, all other things take their proper seats.

This is when peace that passes all understanding is allowed to guard my heart and mind (Phil. 4:6). Christ Jesus has made it so that I can ask God, AT ANYTIME I WANT, to readjust my focus to the point where it pulls the rest of me into the space where I'm resting in the truth that 1.) God loves me. 2.) God speaks to me. 3.) God constantly tells me the truth about everything He shares with me. And He's told me some excellent things, ya'll. This, right here, is deadly to the kingdom of darkness. For, a person who walks about knowingly carrying heaven's by-laws within—understanding how to execute them in the earth—is a force to be reckoned with BECAUSE OF GOD.

So, ain't no good enough reason, really, to renege on the level of relationship that God earnestly wants with us. He's been putting in the work with us since He wrought us, and I now see it as an honor to be elected to let go of what's former in order to latch onto what's present. I'm wrapped up in a God who can masterfully instruct a people to trust Him to annihilate enemies of the past, which causes us to fall madly in love with Him in the now, as He walks us through, on dry land, to what's next.

Feb 28, 2019 — Entry 25 — 5 min read

Peace, Chile!

So, when I was watching the movie *Freedom Writers* with my students yesterday, and I realized I was the only body in the room wanting to get up and dance when Montel Jordan's "This Is How We Do It" came boomin' through my classroom speakers, I realized how much time has passed between the release of this song and now. The age gap between my students and me materialized once again [as it does with each passing year]. I wondered, *What kind of beats drive their boogie today?* And of course, I know the answer to this [because I hear the mess they bump and spout in the building], but it still baffled me as to why Montel's dope beat didn't stir them at all. They just sat like statues watching the screen. And this, my internal rhythm just couldn't understand.

The Bible Tells Me So

From the first time a student ever told me "no," leaving my jaw dropped and on the ground (my first year as a teacher), culture has continued its swift change, and has progressively become what it is. This is no surprise, for the Bible warns about how vultures gathering indicates a carcass is near, and how the branch buds on a fig tree indicate the nearness of Summer. It goes on to advise that one keep watch for the return of Christ because it is not the business of man to know the day or time of this event; however, it is the business of man to find where his purpose lies (Matt. 24). And once he does this, he is to heed every word of the Purpose Giver. In this, one finds the security that is also promised in the Bible. "Now I say to you that you are Peter (which means 'rock'), and upon this rock I will build my church, and all the powers of hell will not conquer it. And I will give you the keys of the Kingdom of Heaven. Whatever you forbid on earth will be forbidden in heaven, and whatever you permit on earth will be permitted in heaven" (Matt. 16:18, 19 NIV). The significance of this is when one knows God in relationship, through Jesus Christ, one is empowered with the by-laws of heaven and the ability to execute them in the earth.

Calling Cunning Intercessors

So, all is definitely not lost just because times have changed [and kids today don't nod their heads to Montel Jordan's "This Is How We Do It"]. If you're a part of the Church of Jesus Christ, you're equipped to live excellently through what looks like hell on earth. And from an intercessory conference prayer call, of which I was a part this morning, Pastor Shawn Stephens encouraged that the signs we're seeing are nothing more than news bulletins confirming how those of us who are cunning in prayer and intercession should be engaged in our craft.

Get In Where You Fit In

With this level of knowledge, the peace that accompanies it is to die for, meaning, in order to attain a level of peace such as this, one must die to self, making it a habitual practice in life. I spoke a message at my church a short while back entitled "I Have Abandonment Issues." The crux of this message is that there is such a thing as good issues of abandonment—when a believer continually and progressively dies to self so that he becomes conditioned to not needing things his way—in order to attain happiness. He learns to be okay with what the Master (God, His Father) wants and the way he fits into this.

Have you ever met a person who just goes with the flow most times? Whenever asked what he wants, what time he'd like to leave, what he desires to eat, or what movie he'd like to see, he mostly responds that it doesn't really matter. And it's not that this type of individual has no backbone, goals, or drive. It's just that he seems to understand what things are worth communicating preference regarding and what things are truly frivolous in the grand scheme. This type of person is a breath of fresh air, a nice change-up from people who always have an opinion about something they just can't let go of until errrrryyyyyybody else sees it the way they do.

First of All

But this can't be so with those of us who desire to walk as closely with God as He desires us to walk with Him. This is because we cannot fulfill the first and great commandment—which is to love Him with all of our heart, soul, mind, and strength—if we're giving Him an earful of what we will and will not do (Deut. 6:5). For, the Bible says that to love Him is to obey Him (John 14:15), and the last time I checked, the one in the relationship who must obey does not call the shots. In order to attain and maintain a high place of peace, one must be fine with pleasing God no matter what. This, my friends, pulls us away from ourselves and encases us in consistent abandonment of our shot-calling tendencies.

This type of posture is making me a cool mom (in my humble opinion). In the times when I want to blow my top at my two testosterone-filled boys (and some days my top does get away from me, chile), abandonment of myself, my temper, my anger, my frustration, and my impatience finds me speaking calm, non-sugar-coated truth to them. Today, they were knocking on the car window from *inside*, as I was pumping gas *outside*, to "tell" on each other. First of all, they acted like they couldn't wait until I got back into the car to tell me these weightless things. Secondly, I asked them, "Is this something you wanna' give up your peace for?" Then and there, I realized I've grown. And in my inquiry to them, I spoke a message to myself—a good evaluative one.

Do Not Disturb

So, this is how *I'm* gonna' do it (Montel). If something that's gonna' make withdrawals from my peace comes along, I'll step aside and let it pass or not allow it into my *sha-nah-nah*, as Gospel Radio Host Willie Moore Jr. likes to say. This level of peace—which I've paid a price for—is not to be disturbed. God's got me in His training program, showing me how to keep my seat.

Mar 23, 2019 — **Entry 26** — 4 min read

Love Said, "Not So!"

I sighed after driving past a couple of wind-tattered bundles of maroon and black weave as they lay, without an owner, in the grassy median on Taylor Ave. Usually, when I see things like this, especially working in an urban school, I deduce that there's been a fight between females whose hair got yanked out. I was pretty confident that this is what happened here on the median although other scenarios are possible as well. I recall a day when I was leaving school, and when I rounded the corner of the first floor, before me was a sea of single braids that obviously once belonged to a female youth. However, because of this sea that I could see, I knew she no longer had them and had become a girl who was walking around covering patches in her head, with a hat or hood, until she could get home to tell her mama what happened—in addition to scheduling a hair appointment STAT!

Maury Who? Jerry Who?

Unbelievable for some? Maybe just a few. But we're in a day when Maury Povich (who's actually still on the air) and Jerry Springer are now amateurs to the violence to which we're privy. Shoot! All we have to do to see ridiculous aggression is scroll through social media. There, we can find somebody's grandmother, in the Dave and Buster arcade, slingin' a 14-year-old girl around by the hair for some type of offense. LORD, HAVE MERCY!

On a weekly basis, I tell my students that I'm allergic to ratchet behavior, to the point where I break out in hives, when it's forced upon me. They think it's funny, but I can even think back to my own high school days when a fight would break out. I would go the opposite way of the fight. I have not been one to thrive off of watching violence, and I have certainly not run toward it. There's something about it that's very irksome to me. So, I guess, when it's come to acts of violence, I've done what the Bible outlines for believers to do with the sightings of evil—and that's flee.

Achy, Breaky Heart

It just does something to my heart to see individuals (outside of organized sport) pounding on each other with the intent to truly and physically harm the other. It's gruesome and devilish. And oh man! When someone has to physically fight to defend oneself! Man! The pits! I mean, who wants to incur a bruised body at any time? And when the beating is brought on by evil and lack of love? Ugh!

This is why the Bible has a first and great commandment that says, "You shall love the Lord your God with all your heart, with all your soul, and with all your mind" (Matt. 22:37). The verse right after it establishes the second greatest commandment, which is to "love your neighbor as yourself." On these two commandments hang everything God cares about. This is critical stuff here, people!

Fuh Real-Fuh Real

Now, the reason, I gather, these two commandments are set up this way is because in order for everyone to have the proper view on how to love another, we first must know what it is to love God. Those of us who know, biblically, that to love God is to obey Him, understand that in aligning ourselves to what He says, in all things, we're going to be groomed regarding how to love others. If we're branches of Christ (John 15:1-8), we ought to be an extension of the way He is. We ought to produce fruit He's proud of having attached to His name. And I'm quite confident that harming another person for spite is NOT His way of doing things.

Sometimes, people bump their heads and think that God loving us means He looks at us as *we* see ourselves and loves the stuff that stinks, helping us to feel better about the way it smells. But BeBe and CeCe Winans sang, "Love said, 'Not So' "—and so do I! Christ IS the better Way, and He wouldn't be the model of perfection that He is if He allowed us to remain the same by "loving" us but overlooking our ratchet-ness. CHILE, PLEASE! We better get over ourselves. We better seek God about how He sees us and the heart posture we must have in order to see the way He sees. Point blank—bottom line—beginning AND end of story.

We dare not go to God and tell Him how He's gonna' love us. We done bumped our heads if we think this God, who *is* LOVE, is gonna' be okay with leaving us to being anything less than who He created us to be. He will not relinquish us to our own dusty devices if we let Him have His way with our love walk. He will take us, polish, and buff us so He can continually see His reflection in our shine.

LOVE says, "Not So ..."

Apr 14, 2019 **Entry 27** *5 min read*

No Vacancy

One recent, late Tuesday night, Kwesi, the boys, and I arrived home from Bible Study to a scene we had not experienced before. There were three foxes frolicking around our immediate area as if they had established, beforehand, to meet at this particular time and place. First, we thought there was only one, which came from our backyard. A few moments later, Kwesi spotted a second one coming from up the street to the right of us. The two began playing in the middle of our street, almost in front of our house. Then adding more to our surprise, a third one joined the party. They were off to the races, down the street a little, darting in and out of our neighbors' yards. We couldn't believe it. Yes, we see stray foxes and rabbits here and there (foxes way less than rabbits), but never have we seen a fox forum of three like this. We all sat in the car for a bit to ensure the foxes were far enough away, allowing us to get into the house. On my way to closing my eyes for bed that night, the fox scene hung around with me because I sensed a message in it.

Deception Waiting in the Ranks

In the bed, I opened my dream interpretation book and read that foxes in dreams represent subtlety and deception. The fact that there were three of them (the number three means "conform/obey") pointed to my need to pay attention to what the Lord was showing us through the foxes. It was a warning against deception infiltrating the state of rest and peace in which our family abides—a heads-up to protect the closer level of intimacy Kwesi and I have reached in our marriage. Seeing the foxes feeling free to run and play around our dwelling place, "trapping" us in our vehicle while they lingered, made this statement. It was such a surreal experience, which challenges me in articulating the seriousness in its nature. And so, since then, I've been praying against any entryways (to what God's built in us) through which the devil could gain access.

Spring Is in the Air

Working in tandem with this warning, God has put a passage in Song of Solomon in my path which says, "Look, the winter is past, and the rains are over and gone. The flowers are springing up, the season of singing birds has come, and the cooing of turtledoves fills the air. The fig trees are forming young fruit, and the fragrant grapevines are blossoming ... [therefore] Catch all the foxes, those little foxes, before they ruin the vineyard of love, for the grapevines are blossoming!" (2:11-13 & 15—NLT).

In this passage, the lovers have been speaking to each other and celebrating their love. The young woman, referring to her beloved as "darling," observes that there's been a change in season and that it adds even more beauty to what she and her man have. The young women of Jerusalem, those who are an audience to these two lovers, wisely admonish them to bind up all the foxes—the subtle stuff that's notorious for interrupting and even destroying the seasonal growth and beauty that surrounds the lovers. Oh, what words of wisdom these are!

Use the Cheat Sheet

So, especially in this season, where I'm running with [and have no plans of retreating from] a much greater appreciation for the privilege of prayer, I take full hold of this warning (through the foxes) that God sat right in our laps. I know He doesn't waste words and that there's always gold behind them. So, when He gives me the answers to the test—and not just in His written Word, but through messages that find me prophetically—I don't want to be the dummy who doesn't use the cheat sheet.

This test within a test falls on a point in a timeline that's leading to another place in God for our family, as we're on the cusp of what hubby and I consider to be a sizable shift in our lives and household. I'm leaving a teaching career of 15 years, and we, as a family, are about to follow God into deeper reaches of the ocean we've been traversing together. Kwesi and I haven't seen eye-to-eye on this thing long—shoot—we were *just* seeing about eye-to-shoulder a few days ago. However, after thinking I've been "Cuckoo for Cocoa Puffs" since (spring of last year) mentioning my God-led consideration and desire of resigning, Kwesi has told God, "It's on You," and has given me the green light regarding this.

Confirmation Nation

I can't count the number of God confirmations I've gotten regarding this shift—prophetic dreams and sermons, conversations that have found me, the select few people I've asked to pray with me (holding me accountable for really hearing God on this), down to two or three sightings of a Mitsubishi ENDEAVOR (knowing good and well I'd never even HEARD of this car before God started talking to me about this shift).

And in this transitional period, where there's an exciting newness of spring in the spiritual air we're breathing, I know Satan would love to snatch, right from under our feet, what we've built around Christ, causing it to come crashing and burning to the ground, leaving a catastrophic scene of destruction where we currently reside. NOPE! AIN'T gonna' HAPPEN, DEVIL. I see you.

William Shakespeare wrote:

"As whence the sun 'gins his reflection
Shipwracking storms and direful thunders break,

So from that spring whence comfort seemed to come
Discomfort swells."

Translated, this means that trouble is compelled and assigned to find a space where there are divinely ordered pleasantries, that it may overshadow and wreck them with countering storms. However, because my God is One of great faithfulness, He's THE constant light that dispels and repels the darkness wherever He shines. So, at this turn in seasons, I'm training my awareness to remain God-centered 24/7 so that no matter what comes, it will find me—find us—properly postured in His provident care.

Make Room

Jonathan McReynolds sings a song entitled "Make Room," which sums up my heart's posture in this moment. The song is about making sure to create space in your life for God, ensuring that He knows He doesn't come second to anything. Some of the lyrics speak of various things in our lives, like our itineraries, our attitudes, our habits, and egos that God can move over and out of the way so that we properly see and set Him where He ought to be. I believe God has seen what He needs to see—in the way I have responded to His hand in my life—through good, bad, and terrifying, and He's been nudging me—with a burning fire—for what's next.

It is my constant expectation of myself that, as I press to live each day most aware of Him, being concerned with His pleasure, I have—no matter the season, bliss, or trial—made it crystal clear to Him that there is a NO VACANCY sign engraved in my heart where He resides.

*This piece was actually completed on February 10, 2019 but was held until a proper time of release.

June 16, 2019 # Entry 28 *5 min read*

Inside Out

"We all have our own stories, each of us drawn by the Spirit in a unique way to the same place of understanding: *God loves me.*" - Mary Jo Pierce

"And may you have the power to understand, as all God's people should, how wide, how long, how high, and how deep *His love is.*" - Ephesians 3:18

EVERYTHING in life boils down to the fact that nothing and no one on this earth—no "other created thing can" top or beat the love of God (Rom. 8:39).

This is freeing, people.

Why?

Because this means that nothing—not the worst thing you can think of, not the deepest and darkest secrets you wish to hide from everyone you think matters, and not the most supreme hurt that anyone or anything has caused you—can truly trump God's love.

It's with His love that He pursues us like a stalker (for righteousness' sake) who just won't quit. It's in His love that He has the patient capacity to pick us up, dust us off, and love away our over-awareness of the things we allow to push Him aside. He shows Himself to us in such a way that He fills the places we thought were more worth our time, focus, and energy.

Kitchen Kismet

It's amazing what happens with us when the way we see life changes while life *itself* doesn't change. The other week, I experienced joy just standing in my kitchen—a kitchen that needs mopping and that houses a ceiling fan currently requiring a good dusting. With no majestic plans on my agenda for the remainder of the evening on this particular day, I was hit by the simple realization that God's teaching me the timeless jewel-of-a-lesson to be content in all things, and I stood there at the counter smiling for—what would appear to anyone who walked in on my moment—no good reason.

I believe many of those in the Bible, who walked closely with, and did super things in the name of God, had this type of awareness tool tucked tightly in their hearts and minds. Therefore, their lives have been recorded in the most popular book on earth.

This leads me to where I currently reside. And at this point, I appreciate the place of godliness with contentment, which puts a rightful damper on the people and instances lined up to damage, deter, and distract me.

Inside Out

Inside Out. Have you seen the movie? It's absolutely adorable and soooooooooooo meaningful. It's about an 11-year-old girl named Riley who moves from a comfy life with her parents in Minnesota to

San Francisco. The movie features Riley's emotional epicenter where we meet the five core emotions that guide her activity in life. There's Disgust, Anger, Fear, Sadness, and Joy, and they're all constantly at play within Riley. All things Riley can be attributed to them.

For example, when Riley starts her new school in San Francisco, the Fear emotion within her goes through several possible first-day failure scenarios as he frantically runs around the headquarters in which he and the other emotions reside. Since Riley's early childhood, her Disgust emotion has freaked out, with much sass, when exposed to things like broccoli or bad smells. Her Anger emotion speaks aggressively, most of the time, and has been known to literally blow his top (spewing fire from his head) when something greatly displeases him. Sadness and Joy struggle the most with each other because Sadness is always ... well ... sad and depressed, and Joy runs herself ragged, trying to keep everything in Riley's life happy and peachy. This leads Joy on a journey to a world-rocking discovery that the other emotions, namely Sadness, also play pivotal roles in Riley's development.

Joy learns that her attempts to stifle them does Riley a disservice, by removing the opportunities for Riley to build meaningful relationships in her life—with her parents, her best friend, her teammates from her hockey team, etc. The over-absorption of what Joy tries to do, putting out every one of Riley's emotional fires, drives away the chance for Riley to make core memories as she navigates *through* the challenges of feeling fearful, sad, angry, and disgusted. When her hockey team in Minnesota lost the championship, her parents were the ones to sit with and comfort her through her tears. This established a warm core memory of their love and availability to her in tough times.

My Point

What I'm building is that the things we go through in life are opportunities for our growth. When we learn how to receive help from the community of people and resources around us, we can create ways to come out of our struggles. We also free ourselves of the burden to save face or appear that we can hold all things together without any help. We basically tell pride NO!

Ultimately, what frees me is that my BIG GOD and FATHER sees me in every moment as I live. He's known me since before I was born. So, do I really think this God of infinite wisdom–the God who IS love, will steer me wrong or leave me stranded in the middle of a process He started? I sometimes hit patches where I fear the familiarity that occurrences from my past want to still have with me, or I fear the unknown particulars of what's to come. However, I know that 1.) God loves me. 2.) God has a purpose for me to serve, and 3.) Dat 'gummit, I'm gonna' serve that purpose!

Clap It Up for These Men!

So, with my resolve to constantly acknowledge my heavenly Father, I highlight this FATHER'S DAY and the men in my life who have been instrumental in my development regarding what I was put on this earth to do.

Thank you, Reverend David R. Montgomery, my father, who's done an earth-shattering and undo-able job of showing me how a man is to love his daughter. I'm thankful for John H. Montgomery, my paternal grandfather, who, I was told, rolled across his bed with glee after I entered the world. Thank you, Clyde L. Rogers, my maternal grandfather, who's **never** missed placing a birthday card for me in the mail these 38 years. Thank you, Cyruss D. Powell Sr., my stepfather, who lovingly took on the challenge of blending a family inclusive of an originally very sassy pre-teen. Thank you, Reverend Dr. W. Raymond Bryant, my to-the-point pastor during my pivotal teenage years of falling in love with God for myself. Thank you, Pastor Lawrence G. Richardson, my pastor during my college years to current, who's taken my thirst for more of God—since I was 18—and has pushed it to levels that have yielded crazy, great rewards.

And thank you to the man who leads and has walked with me for the past 13 years of marriage—the father of my two boys—Mr. Kwesi C. Payne. You, sir, have my respect, love, and devotion to being the best version of the helpmeet for you that God's gonna' continue to help me be. Thank you for your patience.

By the grace of GOD, I am what I am.

(1 Cor. 15:10)

Aug 2, 2019 — **Entry 29** — 4 min read

From Injury to Victory

I used to dread long car rides with my husband because [until recently] I wasn't at complete ease while he drove. Just being honest, chile. But the other day, as we drove down to North Carolina from Maryland to see my dad and stepmom, I realized I've grown to a greater place of appreciation for PROCESS.

Bye Bye, Former Me!

I used to get uptight about our departure times for road trips because I've always wanted to make the most of our time spent away from home. Driving for eight [nerve wrecking] hours or more just to turn around a day later and drive home is not this sista's cup of tea. So, the former me would've awakened (the morning of departure) anxious about the fact that we probably wouldn't leave home until the afternoon. This would've been a crappy alternative to "pushing out" at the wee hours of the morning so we could enjoy some of the day actually in our desired destination (before having to go to sleep for the night right after arriving). Might I add that packing for a vacay requires a certain level of mental commitment and stamina (especially when you're packing with more than just two peeps in mind) that I'm rarely up for?

Anyway, over the past few years, God and I have become closer, and I'm certainly alright with this! The method by which He's chosen to draw us nearer to each other, however, is one I'd not have selected on my own. But [again] learning to appreciate process has been a piece added to the puzzle in this recent portion of my spiritual journey.

God Done Flipped It!

A few years back, seemingly out of nowhere, my mind underwent what felt like mental assault regarding my character and identity. One day, my son and I were watching a movie, and BAM! Thoughts about me (in the middle of the film) being anything other than a child of God began to flood my mind. It was a mess! I thought, *God, what in THE WORLD is going on here???* I began to freak out at these thoughts, and I couldn't get my mental footing for a long while—I'm talking years—because of course, life just kept on churning. And all the while, I was trying to get a solid grip on myself, striving to re-grasp my level of peace as I knew it before this barrage of poor thinking seemingly unleashed on me.

Far from my readiness, in that moment, was the nearby understanding that this was a set-up that could catapult me to where I now find myself. In that space, at that time, I didn't think about the fact that a wilderness God nudges you toward is a training ground waiting to sharpen you as a confident weapon for the sake of all things Kingdom.

In this wilderness, and with some good, professional Christian counseling, I have found that what God has been getting at, all this time, is further anchoring me. He's been showing me that my awareness of His closeness to me—regardless of the fight or scary place—is ground breaking, world changing, and earth shattering.

My penchant is to believe whatever He says and to do whatever He says. I just *cannot* live any other way—I mean truly live. And it only makes sense to wholeheartedly believe everything the One who created me has ever said and ever will say to me.

Stabilization

This is how God has stabilized me throughout my wilderness walk. He's caused me to see that the ability to live with an un-phased disregard for fear, not allowing it to grip me, is the secret to knowing my freedom Christ has provided through acceptance of Him. This is because this posture pushes me to worry about nothing, which is what's instructed in Philippians 4:6,7. As a believer, when remembering not to worry is always at hand, I'm left to trusting in God and the written fact that He really is worthy of my cares and burdens (1 Peter 5:7). It truly is a waste of time [which I could use to know His mind about a thing] to worry. I'm learning how to hunker down and truly put first things first—to be built up in my most holy faith (Jude 1:20), with no false or superficial spiritual muscle for the sake of appearance.

A few years ago, I injured my lower back (which I'm still rehabbing today) from lifting loads too heavy for my physical ability at the time. Having come from years of organized athletics, I was used to being in the weight room and taking my body through the paces of heavy hitting resistance training programs. However, once I graduated from college, I quickly stopped maintaining this level of training. So, when, at some points later on (here and there), I wanted to try and get back to my college body and level of weight training, I went about it too hard and fast. My body was no longer accustomed to the level of fitness I once knew. When I got back into the gym more consistently (after my second child) and tried lifting heavy weight again, somewhere along the way, I messed up my back.

Because I wanted to look the way I did in college, I skipped right over the need to ensure my spine could properly sustain all the weight I was putting on it. I bypassed the need to properly rebuild my level of core strength and balance in order to get to my desired level of physical performance and appearance. With that analogy, I push the message that I've learned to put first things first and go through the right paces of being built up, regardless of what the experience looks like to others or myself. Getting a strong foundation on which to build, and allowing God to put the pieces where He wants, is critical to the sustaining strength of day-in and day-out living within His Kingdom.

I don't call the shots for my life. He does. Because this is the case, I'll build how He tells me to build.

And I'll be stable for it.

Go 'head, God!

Sep 6, 2019 — **Entry 30** — *3 min read*

You Can Win!

"As long as you keep ... your head to the sky ... BE OP-TI-MIS-TIC!"

Ya'll remember that catchy *Sounds of Blackness* tune?!

You know how certain songs push you right into a memory? Someplace. Some time? Some point in your life?

This song makes me think of my mama (because she would play songs by this group) and when I was anywhere between the ages of 10 and 13!

Remembering this song, connected to this time period, brings joy to me. I guess it's because it reminds me of a time when I was a child just living life—pretty much carefree, happy, and taken care of.

God's Hand

If I venture to think further about it, my delight in remembering this time isn't necessarily because all things were perfect. For, in fact, my mom and dad were no longer together; they actually divorced when I was about five years old. Then, when I was around the age of 11, my mom and stepdad decided to marry, and *that* was a new thing I had to get adjusted to.

However, the reason I can look back with pleasure and gratitude now is because I see how God took care of me—of all of us—and that each of us has progressed, thrived, and continued to walk and develop in Him up to this day. And guess what—that's enough, and that's good because that's GOD!

A Facelift for Your Past

What I think I'm getting at [as I type this straight from the heart without premeditation] is that I'm learning to honor the past with all of the imperfections it yields.

I recently heard a pastor preach about people often pegging their pasts with damnation because of some of the hard stuff pasts hold. However, the point he highlighted beautifully is that the things in our pasts [be they good, bad, or disgustingly ugly] are no match to top God at any point. This is because He has the ability to work everything together, in our lives, for good (and not just *our* good). This is why there's nothing that can ever be stamped *FOR LOSS* in God through Jesus.

"In Him also we have obtained an inheritance, being predestined according to the purpose of Him who works all things according to the counsel of His will, that we who first trusted in Christ should be to the praise of His glory" (Eph. 1:11-12 NKJV).

This scripture says, to the believer, that God (even while we were not yet saved) has always had, in His eternal mind, what He's wanted to do in the earth THROUGH our lives. And so, this doesn't encourage us to live lazily around His will (for that isn't the purpose of this passage). What this should spark and feed within us is an affinity to please and obey Him in EVERYTHING we do. We should be fixated on this and driven out of our comfort zones by it.

Shoulders Others Can Stand On

The pastor I have referred to went on to preach that the things and experiences in our pasts are building blocks—if we allow God to test us out of our feelings about the stuff—for somebody else to step on for their spiritual ascension. The notches in our spiritual belts, the scars that have healed [but are recognizable], and the pits we've clawed our way out of, can empower others.

Hallelujah!

So, when God tells us, in His Word, to not fear, to keep our thoughts on Him, to gird up the loins of our minds, to know the simplicity with which we're called to live through obedience to Him, to love Him with all that's within us—

He's—telling—us—to win!

For, if we do these things, we'll be exactly who He crafted us to be, which will blaze trails for the others who have the same responsibility.

Amen.

Sep 14, 2019 — 3 min read

Entry 31

Done Deal

So, somebody let himself into my car somewhere between when I arrived home last evening and my departure this morning—and stole my wallet.

Yes, I've been taking the necessary steps—since the discovery of this *someone's* choice—to ensure that our money and identities remain intact. So far, so good.

As I was walking around my house, thinking about the few other incidents like this that have happened where we live, my mind ran across the following:

There was the time when a car followed us home at night. When we got out of our car, one of the knuckleheads inside it yelled, "Ya'll have a nice night!" (seemingly to intimidate us) and drove off. Then there was the time when someone attempted to break into the house (while no one was home), only to find that though they broke window panes in the door, they couldn't get past the dead bolt. Then there was the other time someone chose to go into one of our cars looking for things. And now—this time.

What dawns on me is that each time, our dwelling place has been found secure. Let me explain.

Knuckleheads Can Teach Too!

The time when the knuckleheads followed us home and told us to have a good night, my first response was, "Oh, no they're not!" And I commenced to pacing within our home—praying aloud—speaking to intimidation and fear that would try and make me crumble.

The time when someone tried to break into the house—welp—they found that they could only do artificial damage to the property.

The first time someone went through the car, they found no wallet, no cash, no nothing (and I'll add they left all the compartments open—guess they ain't care 'bout tidying up—RUDE!).

Oh yeah. I forgot to mention the time my dad and stepmom mailed something to our boys. A neighbor who lives way down the street brought over the opened, wind-blown box that remained after another special someone had invited themselves to the package contents. That time, my boys didn't receive what was intended, by their grandparents, for them to have. But here's the bottom line. They didn't really miss it because they had MORE than enough toys, clothes, and other provisions. That which my dad and stepmom lost in funds pales in comparison to them being able to talk to their grandkids whenever they want!

And this time—I've prayed for the person who made an unethical [but possibly dire] decision to steal my wallet. I've asked God to deal with him/her the way He can and chooses. This wasn't a "Get 'em, God" type of prayer either. I want God to, as I would—had they not taken from me—do whatever He needs to do in that life, pulling the person closer to Him. This is my prayer for all people because at every part of my day, this is my heart posture—that all would be saved.

So, what's been the prevailing factor, as people have tried to negatively/physically/emotionally influence where we live, is the consistent spiritual growth that God has done in us—these Payne people. And I will have it this way until the day I die.

There's an impenetrable anointing that God bestows upon His people who will simply be like children when it comes to Him and them.

Therefore, I'm the kid.

He's the dad.

That's it.

Done deal.

*Top off this piece by listening to "For My Good" by Judah Band.

Dec 21, 2019 — Entry 32 — 4 min read

I Done Learned from the Critters

So, before I left the house today for an accountability session with a friend/ministry teammate, I flushed PL down the toilet. It was a sad, icky sight, chile. SMH–

I found him at the bottom of the tank on his back–lifeless.

He was on his back earlier this morning before the boys and I left the house for school, but when I tossed the fish food in, he flipped over and ate. I thought maybe he was just chillin 'til the vittles came down.

However, the story was over when I got back home from the gym.

Supplement–Not Main Event!

PL (The LATE PL) was the newest member of our fish family (a pleco). He joined the team to help us keep the tank clean a wee bit longer between cleanings since we have three huge goldfish who are quite dirty. But here's yet ANOTHER message that the animal kingdom done taught me–YOU STILL GOTTA' CLEAN THE STINKING TANK!

Changing over to spiritual application here—

1. We must keep our atmosphere clean. We cannot skip critical maintenance. Our lives depend on it.

2. We cannot depend on things, which are intended to only be supplemental, to sustain our spiritual health (all facets of our health, really) by themselves. We must stick to the instructions and regiments that give us the most bang for our buck. And in the case of all humanity, THE SOURCE is God the Father of Jesus the Savior.

3. We cannot be afraid to flush dead things (cuz ya'll know that's where PL went—down the toilet). We need to let go of that which no longer has life to lend—no matter how it made us feel, how it provided comfort to us, how it made us happy, or how it fit nicely at one point.

Infiltration for Education!

The animal kingdom has been really pressing into my moments recently. Do you recall the piece I wrote about three frolicking foxes outside of my home one late night after Bible Study? These foxes were playing in the middle of the street as if they were way out in the country somewhere—a place where there wasn't a lot of traffic, nor were there people moving about. And this struck me oddly because this was [and is still] not a regular occurrence around my neighborhood. Ultimately, the GOD lesson for me (and the Body of Christ) was that we ought to be mindful of the sly, innocent-looking ways (Proverbs 2 refers to them as "little foxes that spoil the vine") that evil lurks to creep into our lives to cause chaotic uprising wherever we dwell.

The way we keep evil from taking over our habitation is by obeying God and remaining in a posture that won't allow us to relent when it comes to doing what brings Him pleasure.

Something that three to four bees (that entered my vehicle—unauthorized through open windows—all different days and times) have taught me is that in life, we must be careful to—when small things that can result in huge spiritual fender benders enter our space—take the critical time to calmly, quickly, and wisely quench them—end them—squash them.

Chile, I'm just tellin' my story! I have one more anecdote for you!

How Did You Get in Here?!?!

I came home from the gym two days ago to find a big black cricket on my kitchen countertop! Mortification quickly visited me, but I got my druthers about me and marched right to get the fly swatter! I began talking to myself in my head saying, *YOU KNOW YOU ONLY GOT ONE SWING CUZ IF YOU MISS, YOU AIN'T gonna' BE ABLE TO FIND IT AGAIN!* And as I swung at it, I found myself mumbling—very sternly under my breath, and tight lipped–expressing that it had the NERVE to be on my kitchen countertop! But I killed it in one FULLY amped swing! Then I had to clean it up with a paper towel, cleaner, and such.

My point, believers, is that we gotta' keep guard over our entryways and lives. The Bible says that we have to diligently keep watch over what gets into our hearts because the issues that we see coming from us start right there (Prov. 4:23).

These days, when I'm riding in my car with the windows down, I'm watching closely because I don't want any unwelcome critters flying, buzzing, or creeping in.

This stands to be so with my walk. I'm watching my ports and am praying the same for the Body of Christ because we're supposed to be the ones who help others find Him. It's not that we have to be perfect (because this will never happen on this side of heaven); however, our hearts are only safe in the hands of the Lord. If we leave them exposed to that which is threatening to our purity, we'll find that all kinds of things will come to disrupt, inhabit, and feast on our souls in order to thwart our effectiveness in the Kingdom.

I'm just sayin'.

June 13, 2020 **Entry 33** *3 min read*

When the Boys Come Knockin'

It's 9:36 Saturday morning, and I'm just committing to waking up. My husband's been up for a bit and is now downstairs. Before leaving the room, he made sure the comforter was pulled up around me nicely and then left.

I Shouldn't Have Assumed

I've been more tired than usual since I've been getting up early to work on some things without being pulled on by anyone for a few hours (wives and mamas, ya'll know what I'm talkin' about). Well, I assumed my sons understood why they haven't seen me surface downstairs yet this morning. I assumed they understood why my bedroom door was still closed. And I assumed that they respected this reason. However, moments ago, the persistent knocks of my five-year-old gently rapped on my door. When they went unanswered, he went away—the first time. But when they started up for the second round, I finally said, "Come in" (in a groggy voice). And you know what? I can't even remember what he asked me when he came in to talk to me because I was still quite tired.

About 15 minutes later, the knocks of my nine-year-old came. With courtesy, he said good morning and proceeded to ask me if I'd read the note (written in purple crayon) he left on my pillow on his way to bed last night (the note was about the purchase of a Nintendo Switch). I appreciate the gentle nature he carried when he interrupted my Saturday morning snooze; however, I knew that both boys had come knocking without their father knowing their actions. I believe their attempts would have been intercepted had my husband known their agendas.

He Loves Me

I believe this because my husband left me asleep with the understanding that I needed more rest. I believe he had the heart to let me sleep while he went downstairs to start the day's parenting alone. I believe he didn't disturb me because he loves me and wants to show me. And so, in this sense, he selected to cover me, taking on the tasks of making breakfast and supervising our boys, granting me the chance for extra rest. Again, had he known the boys had it on their minds to come knocking on my door to interrupt my sleep, he would've stopped them.

God's Classroom

This causes me to think of how I've been learning more about God and the way He takes care of His children. Those who don't care to know Him may think that if He's so good, He won't allow anything bad or gut wrenching to come to those He loves. And some Christians may start their walk with

Him thinking similarly while moving toward the interesting reality that bad times don't equal His nonchalance regarding His loved ones.

What they do equal is the truth that He's sovereign and perfect in His ways. What they do teach us is to trust Him with our lives. The notice they do serve us is that at the core of our bond with Him is the requirement of our love *for* Him *through* obedience *to* Him (John 14:15). So, when He lifts up His guard gate to allow bad stuff through—when He allows life interruptions to come knock at our door—it's to bring us to another level of awakening and truth about who He is and who we are. Therefore, it's for our good to learn not to despise fiery situations and disruptions that jolt us awake.

Believe and Obey

It's the job of His children to:

1. BELIEVE that He loves us (and that there's nothing that'll ever change that, for if that could be changed, then who He is could be changed) - 1 John 4:8,19
2. Respond in OBEDIENCE to Him through it ALL. This is how we give love back to Him and serve our purpose in life. Living any other way is a waste of time (and we all know that time eventually runs out).

So—when "the boys" come knocking, stay at rest in who God is and the fact that He loves you.

June 18, 2020 — **Entry 34** — *3 min read*

Speak to My Heart

Speak to my heart, Lord.
Give me Your holy Word.
If I can hear from You, then I'll know what to do.
I won't go alone.
I'll never go on my own.
Just let Your Spirit guide
And let Your Word abide.
Speak to my heart, Lord.

These lyrics swell inside one of my favorite songs (come through, Donnie McClurkin!) which takes me back to the early days of my faith.

1998! Morgan State!

I start thinking of freshman year—Morgan State—Blount Towers—the eighth floor with my roommate LaShawn! During these days, I'd started a fresh chapter in life and was newly on fire for the Lord. My heart beamed with excitement to get closer to God and do what He said. I loved reading the Bible, discovering these beautifully untouchable yet simple truths that applied to me and made me feel so powerful. These were truths that made me feel like flying as I'd walk across campus to and from class, knowing I was a King's kid who really wanted to please Him. These kinds of memories make me smile. I was 18 years old, young, athletic, and a great catch who had her head on straight with her heart pointed in the right direction. To top it all off, I stumbled into a relationship with a ministry that rocked my young world, opening doors to the next level type of faith I panted for! It was **on and poppin'** (this phrase still lingers today, yes?) for my young life.

It's DOPE Still

No, I wasn't naive to the fact that life had never been and would never be perfect, but THIS CHRISTIAN THANG WAS DOPE! Twenty-two years later, I look up from a more seasoned state and am happy that I can still say the same.

This Christian thang is dope.

Of course, less-than-desired occurrences done happened because such is life, but through what I've seen, I still end up better for it. And guess what—so do others who come into contact with me!

Do I have weak moments? Yes! Though, in these weak moments, where have I learned to QUICKLY run? **GOD**!

After miscarriage number one, who was I voicing my frustrations to? **GOD**! In the course of 15 years, when high school kids sometimes cussed at me, challenged my authority, and made it way less than pleasant to teach them, whose face was I in? **GOD'S!** When our little red Mazda MX-3 spun out of control on I-95 en route to my folks' home in VA, who did I thank as my heart palpitations died down? **JESUS!** After miscarriage number two, who did I know could hold my hand through yet another loss of a baby? Who could I thank for the two kids who have my last name and are well today? **MY FATHER!** Who do I, sooner rather than later, ask to check my heart for bad stuff when my husband and I have a spat (and I'd rather not close my mouth before more daggers are spoken?) **GOD.**

Who?

Who never sleeps?
Who's always able?
Who made me?
Who made you?
Who knows how this'll turn out?
Who don't you have to be perfect for?
Who sees you in your ratchet-ness and always has solutions to help it?
Who has THE game plan for your life?
Who has THE blueprint for your mind?
Who knows how you should spend your time?
Who's BIG and BAD enough to hold His own?
Who's never been born and never will die?
Who's real regardless of who thinks He is or isn't?
Who does everyone have to answer to, at some point, whether they serve Him or not?

Yup—**GOD.**

So, I repeat—

Speak to my heart, Lord.
Give me Your holy Word.
If I can hear from You, then I'll know what to do.
I won't go alone.
I'll never go on my own.
Just let Your Spirit guide
And let Your Word abide.
Speak to my heart, Lord.

*Suggested song: Donnie McClurkin's "Speak to My Heart"

July 9, 2020 Entry 35 *1 min read*

Feelings Don't Change Truth

Feelings don't change truth
So why go over the deep end?

Feelings don't change truth
So why indulge in my down-in-the-dumps mood?

Feelings don't change truth
So why can't I have the courage of my convictions?

(Just because I'm scared doesn't mean I can't stick to my guns)

Feelings don't change truth
So why can't I fly?

Feelings don't change truth
So why won't I let this bitterness die?

Feelings don't change truth
So, what good's my unforgiveness doing anyone?

Feelings don't change truth
So, I better get up and get movin' before today is done

Feelings don't change truth
So, who cares that they don't like me?

Feelings don't change truth
So, when am I gonna' push through?

Feelings don't change truth
So, why does this still bother me?

(If I focus on the truth
I can move from stuck to free)

Feelings don't change truth
Yes, I do have them

But feelings don't change truth
So, I have to live beyond them

Feelings don't change truth
No, this doesn't mean *run over me*

"Feelings don't change truth" simply means I can always be free from—

Letting my feelings dictate what's true instead of the Truth that's God

My feelings don't change truth
So, I have to get beyond this being odd
Because God'll always be the Truth
Have the truth
Speak the truth
And love the truth

So, I better love the truth
Speak the truth
Have the truth
And honor the TRUTH that is—
Was—
And is to come—

July 28, 2020 — *Entry 36* — 2 min read

Proof

May your struggles keep you near the cross
May your troubles show that you need God
May your battles end the way they should
May your bad days prove that God is good
May your whole life prove that God is good

What beautiful words written to identify with those who have imperfect days, imperfect seasons, and imperfect moments—all of humanity. Jonathan McReynolds was dead on when he wrote these. And I assume he was able to do so from the truth that is his own life.

How freeing it is to know that the life canvas we'd hoped would be spotlessly pristine actually has warps and tears, and holes, and stray marks all over it. And yes, there were impasses where we could've made better choices—choices that would have prevented some of the marks—but there are other blemishes that are there because God knows His creations need hard stuff in order to peel back the layers of who we are.

So, I'm grateful for the scars I have, ONLY because God [and only God] can use them as proof that He can take a mess and beautify it. He can recover misspent energy and time, and tears, and funds, and words, and so on.

He's the MASTER recover-er, and I will not foolishly live as if He isn't the only One.

Yes, my struggles will keep me near the cross.
Yes, my troubles, indeed, show me I need God.
Yes, my battles will end the way they should because I know that
My bad days will prove that God is good.

I vow to Him [in each day–through each moment] that my whole life will prove that He is good.

*Suggested song: Jonathan McReynolds' "God Is Good"

Sep 11, 2020 — *Entry 37* — 2 min read

Greatness Holds Us Accountable

Chile, one of my personal training clients texted me the other day, telling me that her co-worker told her she (my client) inspired her to start working out because of my client's physical transformation over these months. My client said her co-worker told her she (the co-worker) now walks several miles a day and is down 34 pounds since being inspired.

I joked with my client—whose hard work has turned the heads of many others, pushing them to make positive fitness changes—that her greatness, one way or another, will hold her accountable. Her response to me was, *LOL yeah yeah.* However, that stone-cold truth just flowed right from my thumbs, onto my phone, and right into my contemplative space because chile, that is so right and true!

God, the Creator, made everyone—you, me, the sanitation worker, the teacher, the dancer, the phlebotomist, the person on the corner holding the sign, the seemingly homeless man asking for help outside of Dollar General—He made us all to be great. That's why He put it inside of us in the form of talents, gifts, callings, and such. He wants it on display FOR HIS GLORY AND REPUTATION—not necessarily ours.

So, that being said, we might as well go right on 'head and be great. How do we do this? By telling Him yes to everything He has to say and request of us. When we consider the fact that He made us (Genesis 1-3), this question rings strongly: Who are we to ever tell him *no*? The reality is, and will always be, that we have no business doing this, and we need to own up to it. There's really no nice way to say it. We must obey Him because life outside of obedience to our Creator is a waste of time.

I have none to waste, and neither do you. Our time here is limited, and we will all have an eternity to which we must answer. I know which eternity I want knocking at my door, and while I'm here, I want to make all things—all choices count for righteousness.

No one is perfect, and what gives me comfort and rest is that God's not asking us to be. He wants availability, through which He will do super things!

Go on 'head and be great! You're being held accountable to this task anyway, whether you recognize it or not. Your greatness is holding you accountable through that conversation you just had, and you know God was speaking. It's holding you accountable through your child, who just called you to the carpet when you lied in front of him. It's holding you accountable through that commercial you just randomly caught on the TV or radio. It's holding you accountable through remembering what somebody said to you or some situation that happened. It's looking for you to respond with a constant yes. So, utter it and move in obedience.

*Suggestion: Watch "I'm JUHST Sayin" Segment #14 *(Greatness Holds Us Accountable)* on Juhst Bee's YouTube channel! Please like and subscribe!

Dec 13, 2020 **Entry 38** *2 min read*

Friends Are Dope

"I never thought Charles would really stick in my life," I told Kwesi this morning. The way Charles and I met, on the age-old social medium Black Planet, some 22 years ago, never screamed, *This guy will be your friend 22 years from now.* But as time has passed, through various seasons in each of our lives—college, courting, entrepreneurship, marriage, divorce, children, miscarriage, losing long-time loved ones, and now a pandemic—we've kept in touch, and I see how we really care for each other.

Remember When?

Yesterday, it felt good, as Kwesi, Charles, and I tried remembering the different times we've seen each other, and what year this and that happened. I realized how many attempts we've made to keep up with each other, separated by state lines and all. This speaks well of friendship.

I know life happens in seasons, and as I mature, I'm learning to appreciate what I get to learn in each one. God's teaching me compassion and patience with life and my development through it.

In turn, I'm able to appreciate people and relationships on a greater, more enriching level; and for this, I'm thankful. I could imagine what life would be like without God leading the way, but I don't really want to because it would end as a nightmare—even if it was dressed with opulence and seemingly good things.

Physically Distanced Reunion

So, after hanging out in a park down the street from our house—trying to ignore the fact that the nice Baltimore day had swiftly shifted to abruptly cool, and laughing at the fact that Charles doesn't understand why dirt bikes are even a thing here in Baltimore since "it ain't no dirt" here [as he put it]—the boys, Kwesi, Charles, his lovely lady, Maisha, and I headed back to the house, took a physically distanced selfie outside, and parted ways. For the few hours we were in each other's' company, I felt so cool for having a friend—of several seasons—who would bring himself and his lady out of the way to come "kick it" with Kway and me, with the short time they had remaining here in Maryland.

Friends are dope!

Dec 20, 2020 — **Entry 39** — *4 min read*

Seasons Teach

Ummm ... I just passed Santa on a sleigh cycle at a gas station.

It's one of those sights that make you go hmmm...

It made me ask, "Who is that? And WHERE is he going?" And as I'm typing this in a library parking lot, not even five minutes after seeing Sleigh Cycle Santa, a lady with a Santa hat has walked up to the book drop to return some books.

Is there a special convention happening 'round here at this time?

Ha!

Then, preparing to leave the library parking lot, I've turned my music back on, only to be reminded that I've been bumpin' R. Kelly's "Christmas, I'll Be Steppin'" on repeat.

I guess all signs are pointing to a certain theme and time! A time when it makes sense to see a Sleigh Cycle Santa, a random lady wearing a Santa hat, oodles of Christmas lights, decorations, and snow-covered lawns. Duh, Nikk! It's the middle of December!

Did Somebody Say "Up Chuck"???

Much like seasons bring certain signs and call for certain progressions, I know most are familiar with an experience as unpleasant as up chucking (I know this feels like a jump, but just stick with me so I can bring this piece full circle). You know you're gonna' up chuck when your stomach doesn't feel right; then your mouth gets uncontrollably watery, right? You do what you can to keep the flood gates closed, but still, up and out it comes, yes? I've hated those times because there's really nothing you can do but just let things take their course so you can get to the other side of the grossness.

Well, such is life.

I'm Still Hurting

Kwesi and I talked about some things this morning, which I found that I was still hurting about. The cool part was that I didn't try to cover up the fact that the pain was there, once I realized it. I tuned in to what Kwesi was saying to try and help me understand the parts I could've played in the different situations going sour. It didn't feel good, and I kind of wanted to rush through the process I was internally experiencing, to get to the other side (much like the up-chucking experience). But as I cried through it, I was glad that my inner response was also accompanied by my direct plea to God, asking Him to help my heart. I didn't want to hold on to any ill feelings toward anybody involved in these matters—including no ill feelings toward myself for being a possible part of the problem.

So, as the morning continued, and my family prepared for breakfast downstairs, I got up to join in, trying not to be the Debbie Downer of the bunch, but to be as natural and honest in my inner dealings while staying present with the activities of the moment.

Stay Present

This whole "stay present" counsel is actually a thing, I'm finding. I've heard others encourage those who have been grieving, or depressed, or anxious to "stay present," and I'd never really given much thought to its grave importance. However, recently, I've found myself purposely staying present so that I don't give anxiety the satisfaction. It's been doing well for me.

I've also been hearing God deal with me about why this is a thing, and it's come forth that when we remain present—not allowing ourselves to sulk in regrettable past events or be afraid of future moments—we ride nicely in the pocket of the here and now. And for the believer, our here and now rests in the hand of God. It's like a child (in an ideal situation) not having to worry about what clothes he's gonna' wear or what his next meal will be—he just goes about his day, knowing that he's been entrusted to adults who love and will care for him and his needs. I don't hear my children asking me about how much our bills are or how the budget is looking for the month. This is because they don't have to care about these things yet. They're kids being kids!

And when I can take and keep this posture, knowing that I'm God's kid and that His plans for and mind toward me are just what they need to be, I can honestly relax and trust Him to guide me appropriately.

So, when things occur that I don't understand, or when circumstances and relationships get sticky, where—in my mind—I had no ill intent regarding, I have to trust that staying present with God will keep me walking as I should, being as I should, thinking as I should, and loving as I should.

Oops! Upside Yuh Head

The signs, indicators, and landmarks on the highway through life will slap us upside the head every now and then; however, staying present with God will, at some point, align some of these things so we can see where they were pointing all the time. And the other ones that we may never quite be able to put together—well, that'll just have to be well with our souls because we're not all-knowing anyway. We know who is, though.

So, the next time you see a [metaphorical] Sleigh Cycle Santa or feel a [metaphorical] up chuck swelling, keep your eyes open and your heart in the hands of **The Righteous Handler**. He'll ensure that—when necessary—you'll be able to reckon with the indicators, themes, and timing He wants to make clear to you. This will not just be for your sake, but for the sake of others too.

Merry Christmas.

Dec 23, 2020 — **Entry 40** — 4 min read

Game Changer

I almost came to tears as I listened to "O Holy Night" the other day. It was the version from *The Best Man Holiday* soundtrack, when Jayda Brown and Jasmine Watkins made it a duet. I guess I emoted because their voices sounded so pure and childlike. I could tell they had a natural talent to sing, but their voices were still mousy and new. It just expressed such innocence to me.

Then I listened closely to the words–

Long lay the world in sin and error pining, (We needed help)
'Till he appeared and the soul felt its worth. (We had a Savior who could help make sense of who we were meant to be)
A thrill of hope the weary world rejoices (Peeps had something in which to hope)

Chorus
Fall on your knees, Oh hear the angel voices (Do what the angels do & worship Him)
O night divine. O night when Christ was born (The game changer is here)
O night, O holy night, O night divine (Game changer ...)

**words in parentheses are mine*

Bare Bones–Bottom Line

These words express the bare bones of the opportunity, afforded to people of the weary world, to choose a Savior who could save and restore them to the relationship God intended to have with His creation.

And through Jesus, this is as simple as believing that He came for this reason and saying it with them flappers on your face (see Romans 10, 9 & 10).

Then, when it comes to understanding who we are and why we're here, it makes sense to ask the One who made us, yes? This is called conversation with God, AKA prayer. And as I listened to Pastor David Wilford of All Nations Worship Assembly (Chicago West Campus), and he spoke of prayer not being something God intended to feel obligatory to us, but a relational method of communication from Father to child and vice versa, my insides said "Yes!"

Simplify

I find myself talking to God in a similar manner to how I talk to my dad (also named David). If I'm confused, I say, "God, I'm confused." If I'm sad, I say, "Father, I'm sad." If I'm mad, I say, "Lord, help me to close my mouth before I say something to make things worse."

God hasn't set out to make life with Him complicated at all. The Bible speaks of the way to heaven as "a plain way" and "those knowing but little, and unlearned, shall be kept from missing the road" (Matthew Henry Commentary). What, in fact, complicates things between us and Him is when we don't want to do what He wants us to do. We have a problem with the big 'O'. Yep. We struggle with O-B-E-D-I-E-N-C-E. It's our will versus His.

But, in the Third Epistle of John, the apostle writes to his friend Gaius and wishes that Gaius' physical health would be rich like his (Gaius') spiritual health. This scripture has held my attention for years because who doesn't want good health? Who wants to be sick, disabled, or in physical pain? No one I know. The apostle is sending his friend encouragement that he's not only thinking of him but that he understands the dynamic relationship between prosperity of the soul and the physical body.

Barking Up All the Wrong Trees

However, here's what gets overlooked by the majority. Many wish for physical and material prosperity without prosperity of the soul. And yes, today, there are several paths people take to try and enrich their souls to fulfillment; consequently, we go off target in pursuit to make anything a god outside of the One who created the soul. Many are taking shots in the dark when the bullseye is the most LIT there is, ever was, and ever will be. "I am the way, the truth, and the life. No one can come to the Father except through me," says Jesus in John 14:6. The thing is that folks are so busy doubting this, which is a waste of time. Of course, God's the only One who can redeem wasted time, but I'd rather not require this of Him—I'd rather obey the first go-around.

If we get on board with Him from the jump, and walk in alignment with what He wants, we can sit in prayer with more of a relational posture versus the obligatory one. We'll want to come to our *Father* because He's our Father and not because we have to. We'll pant for knowing what He wants us to know, and how He wants us to see things so we don't waste time, thought, energy, or resources. Instead of worrying, I wish to simply ask Him how I should think about the thing that tempts me to fret. Here's where I believe we can start to conquer fear.

So, when you "fall on your knees," let it be out of relationship with your Father and not obligation. How do you get here? Start with the *big* 'O' in the *small* things. This, indeed, will change the game and the player in you.

www.ingramcontent.com/pod-product-compliance
Lightning Source LLC
Chambersburg PA
CBHW071538040426
42452CB00008B/1057

* 9 7 8 1 7 3 6 3 6 4 9 9 4 *